STAGECRAFT IN EURIPIDES

Stagecraft in **Euripides**

MICHAEL R. HALLERAN

CROOM HELM
London & Sydney

© 1985 Michael R. Halleran
Croom Helm Ltd, Provident House, Burrell Row,
Beckenham, Kent BR3 1AT
Croom Helm Australia Pty Ltd, First Floor, 139 King Street,
Sydney, NSW 2001, Australia

British Library Cataloguing in Publication Data
Halleran, Michael R.
    Stagecraft in Euripides.
    1. Euripides — Dramatic production
    I. Title
    882'.01   PA3978
    ISBN 0-7099-1273-0

Typeset by Leaper & Gard Ltd, Bristol
Printed and bound in Great Britain by
Biddles Ltd, Guildford and King's Lynn

CONTENTS

Preface

Acknowledgements

To Erin and in Memory of my Parents

PREFACE

At what point an entering character became visible to the audience is uncertain. In this study a character is said to enter when he speaks his first line or at the line following the announcement, if there is one, of him (or the group he is with), whichever is relevant or comes first, since it is at this point that the character can establish contact with those on stage. A character's exit is often more difficult to determine. Various factors severally or jointly can indicate it, and sometimes it is clear that a character has exited only retrospectively. In general a character is said to exit at the conclusion of the scene of which he was a part, after lines which claim or point to an exit, or before lines which the character cannot be imagined to hear, except, of course, for asides.

For reasons of economy I have avoided the use of Greek in the text and notes, relying on translations and transliterations. I intend the former only to be serviceable, and accordingly I have tried to make them literal and corresponding, in so far as it is possible, to the colometry of the Greek.

With the exceptions of a few, Greek names have been transliterated rather than Latinised. The plays are referred to with abbreviations which should be self-explanatory.

This work has profited from many other studies. Some, because they are cited frequently, are referred to by the name of the author alone:

Bodensteiner, E. *Szenische Fragen über den Ort des Auftretens und Abgehens von Schauspielern und Chor im griechischen Drama*, Jahrb. f. class. Philol. Suppl. Bd. 19 (1893), 637–808

Hamilton, R. 'Announced Entrances in Greek Tragedy', *HSCP* 82 (1978), 63–82

Hourmouziades, N. *Production and Imagination in Euripides: Form and Function of the Scenic Space*, Greek Society for Humanistic Studies, Second Series, vol. 5 (Athens 1965)

Kranz, W. *Stasimon: Untersuchungen zu Form und Gehalt der griechischen Tragödie* (Berlin 1933)

Mastronarde, D. *Contact and Discontinuity: Some Conventions of*

Speech and Action on the Greek Tragic Stage (Berkeley and Los Angeles 1979).

Taplin, O. *The Stagecraft of Aeschylus: The Dramatic Use of Exits and Entrances in Greek Tragedy* (Oxford 1977).

The text of Euripides that I cite or translate is the *OCT* (Murray for vols. 1 and 3, Diggle for vol. 2), except for the following:

Euripide: Les Bacchantes, ed. J. Roux (Paris 1970), vol. 1

Euripides: Hecuba, ed. S. Daitz (Leipzig 1973).

Euripides: Helena, ed. R. Kannicht (Heidelberg 1969), vol. 1

Euripides: Hippolytos, ed. W.S. Barrett (Oxford 1964).

Euripides: Medea, ed. D.L. Page (Oxford 1938).

The fragments are cited from the editions as indicated. For Aischylos and Sophokles I refer to Page's *OCT* (1972) and Dawe's Teubner text (1975–9) respectively.

ACKNOWLEDGEMENTS

An earlier version of this work was submitted as a doctoral dissertation to the Department of the Classics at Harvard University in May 1981. I would like again to thank my dissertation director, Ruth Scodel, for numerous improvements and suggestions, my two readers, Albert Henrichs and Gregory Nagy, for their careful reading, which saved me from many errors and infelicities, and Ralph Rosen for his comments on the first three chapters. In preparing the present work, I was aided by Oliver Taplin's criticisms on a draft of the *Herakles* section in Chapter 5 and Leah Rissman's suggestions on the entire final copy. It is a pleasure to thank them both. An award from Connecticut College's Faculty Research and Travel Grants in 1982–3 assisted me in research, and Ingrid Pearson did the lion's share of typing the final manuscript. I would like also to thank William McCulloh, who first taught me Greek, and the late Cedric Whitman, with whom I began my study of Euripides. I owe much to both men. Finally, I warmly thank my wife, Erin, who gave much of her time and energy in helping with this project in countless ways from the very first to the very last stages. To Erin and in memory of my parents I dedicate this book.

University of Washington
Seattle, Washington

1 INTRODUCTION

Dramatic technique is not a new field of inquiry; in the last century especially it has received considerable study. Individual features of tragedy have been examined,[1] and scholars have given their attention to the visual aspects and staging of these dramas.[2] In recent years several impressive studies of dramatic technique have appeared, including Oliver Taplin's *The Stagecraft of Aeschylus*. In addition to observing various patterns of the tragic stage and offering interpretive remarks on the individual plays, Taplin argued persuasively for his proposed structure of Greek tragedy. The basic structural pattern, according to this theory, consists of not only the alternation of speech and song, but this alternation tied up with the rearrangement of characters by exit(s) before the songs and entrance(s) after them. Many variations of this pattern occur, but its essence seems correct.

All these studies have made strides towards establishing a 'grammar of dramatic technique', to use Eduard Fraenkel's famous phrase, and this grammar has enhanced our understanding of the plays' dramatic language. Although the ancient texts do not contain stage directions,[3] they do refer to and imply stage actions. Studying the texts reveals many patterns of action and conventions of the genre, which provided a framework for the playwright's composition and the audience's expectations. The conventions or 'grammatical rules' are not ironclad; the occasional exceptions to the frequently repeated patterns prove the rule. The object in formulating these conventions is to see the plays in the proper context of the demands and nature of the genre and the audience's expectations. What the audience observed intuitively over time, we observe through study. Knowledge of these conventions and the ways in which the playwright works with and manipulates them contributes to our understanding of the dramas as they were meant to be understood — in performance.

This study builds on and contributes to the 'grammar of dramatic technique' by examining three aspects of it in Euripides: (1) entrances and their announcements; (2) preparation for and surprise in entrances; (3) dramatic connections between exits and entrances and the lyrics that they frame.

Entrances and exits are the most fundamental stage actions. They begin and end scenes, and they most directly bring characters to and remove them from our attention. Studying the patterns and conventions of entrances and exits, we can observe the basic structure and movements of the dramas. In particular, in Chapter 2 I will be examining the relationship between entrances and their announcements. Already work has been done on this aspect of Euripidean stagecraft,[4] but the 'rules' proposed need further modification and refinement. Even more important, the exceptions (real and apparent) to these 'rules' need to be accounted for. The conventions that obtain for entrance announcements prove, in fact, to be closely followed by Euripides, and when he deviates from the normal patterns the anomaly can almost always be explained on structural or dramatic grounds. The anomalies and the reasons for them further inform us about Euripidean dramaturgy and about the individual scenes of the plays. Related discussions, including ones on Euripides' handling of the gods in his dramas, develop.

Drama, especially Euripidean drama, plays on the audience's expectations. Chapter 3 looks at the ways in which Euripides, playing on the audience's expectations, employs surprise entrances. Rarely is the effect of a surprise entrance just a bracing stage action; it is usually important to our understanding of the drama. Euripides surprises us to make a point — to underline some action, to suggest a contrast, or to shift the focus of the drama.

The lyrics of Greek tragedy have been the source of constant study. Walther Kranz published his monumental work fifty years ago, and there remains much to be done in this area. My object in Chapter 4 is to consider the specific dramatic links between the lyrics and the following entrances and the preceding exits, the connections at the major structural junctures of the plays. How does the lyric prepare us for and link itself to what follows with the next entrance? How is a song connected to the preceding exit? Dramatic and thematic purposes are not easily separated. Nor should they be, since the two work together. We focus on these links not only to observe Euripidean dramatic technique but to illuminate the larger issues of the dramas.

Dramatic technique can be studied only over a large corpus. Parallels must be examined and cited for patterns and conventions to emerge. I consider the evidence from all of Euripides' extant tragedies, except the doubtful *Rhesos*. Evidence from the fragments, often of uncertain value, is cited only when particularly relevant either in lending support to or casting doubt upon the material from the extant plays. The dramas of Aischylos and Sophokles are not considered except occasionally when they provide the nearest parallel. Although most of Euripides' works has been lost, the extant seventeen tragedies provide substantial evidence. When so much material has been lost, statements about conventions and patterns may be suspect, but frequently the numbers are overwhelming or at least very suggestive. We can also take comfort in the survival of the 'alphabetic' plays, plays not selected by a later critic. In our discussions the term convention is used when the evidence seems quite conclusive.

In Chapter 5 three plays are discussed in greater detail to show most clearly the rewards of our inquiry. The discussion of these plays is not a complete account of Euripides' dramatic technique in the dramas or a comprehensive literary analysis; it looks at the plays from the perspective of entrance and exit patterns and conventions, our expectations about them, and the links between these important stage actions and the lyrics. Looking at a play in its entirety, we can also observe patterns and dramatic 'echoes' within the drama. I choose for fuller study *Herakles*, *Troades*, and *Ion*. All three plays are from the same period, what Zielinski termed the 'free style' metrically, and perhaps were written within five or six years of each other. Working with plays from the same era seems preferable to selecting 'representative' plays from different ones. And these plays are individually compelling and collectively reflect the dramaturgical abilities and virtuosities of the playwright. They represent, I think, not the calm waters before the storm of *Orestes* and *Bakchai*, but rather the lightning before the thunder.

Notes

1. Among the works I have in mind are: F. Leo, *Der Monolog im Drama: Ein Beitrag zur griechisch-römischen Poetik*, Abh. Ges. Wess. Göttingen phil-hist. Kl. N.F. 10, 5 (Berlin 1908); W. Schadewaldt, *Monolog und Selbstgesprach: Untersuchungen zur Formgeschichte der griechischen Tragödie*, Neue Philologische Untersuchungen 2 (Berlin 1926); W. Nestle, *Die Struktur des Eingangs in der attischen Tragödie* (Stuttgart 1930); W. Kranz, *Stasimon: Untersuchungen zu Form und Gehalt der griechischen Tragödie* (Berlin 1933); J. Duchemin, *L'AGΩN dans la tragédie grecque*² (Paris 1968).

2. See, e.g., J. Dingel, *Das Requisit in der griechischen Tragödie* (Diss. Tübingen 1967) and W. Steidle, *Studien zum antiken Drama, unter besonderer*

Berücksichtigung des Bühnenspiels (Munich 1968).

3. On the issue of stage directions, see recently, Taplin, 'Did Greek Dramatists Write Stage Instructions?', *PCPS* n.s. 23 (1977), 121–32.

4. Especially the studies of Hourmouziades and Hamilton.

2 ENTRANCES AND ANNOUNCEMENTS

A familiar feature of Greek tragedy is the announcement of a character's entrance ('I see the herald approaching'). But not all entrances in Greek tragedy are preceded by such an announcement. In *Alk.*, e.g., the chorus announces (507–8) Admetos' entrance from the palace, while shortly before (476) Herakles arrived on stage unannounced. Why does one character receive an announcement and the other not? An attempt to answer this and related questions illuminates both the conventions of Greek tragedy and the scenes in individual plays.

Over the years scholars have posited various theories to account for the use of entrance announcements in Greek tragedy. They have suggested, among other things, that the crucial factor in determining whether an announcement precedes an entrance or not was the need for identification, the rank of the character, or the element of surprise. Richard Hamilton recently has refuted these theories: characters who have already appeared on stage are announced, while others make their initial appearance with no announcement; both servant and sovereign enter announced and unannounced; and not all surprising entrances lack announcement, nor are all unannounced ones surprising.[1] Another theory claimed significance for the place of entrance — *parodos* or *skene* — but this too does not survive an examination of the texts.[2]

The use of announcements, however, was neither arbitrary nor haphazard. They follow several marked patterns. In particular, one convention and its converse go a long way towards explaining the presence or absence of an entrance announcement: if an entrance immediately follows an uninterrupted strophic song, it is not announced; otherwise, it receives an announcement.[3] Thus in the examples above from *Alk.*, Admetos receives an announcement and Herakles does not.

Significantly this practice is not an isolated phenomenon but, rather, corresponds to a fundamental pattern of Greek tragedy. Oliver Taplin has made a strong case that the basic structural pattern of Greek tragedy is the alternation of speech and song tied up with the rearrangement of characters by exit(s) before the song and entrance(s) after it: enter actor(s) — actors' dialogue — exit

5

actor(s)/choral strophic song/enter new actor(s) etc.[4] Since a song is usually followed by an entrance, that entrance is expected and generally needs no announcement. Because the placement of an entrance that occurs between odes is not predictable, it is usually indicated by an announcement, which is one way of alerting those on stage, and the audience, of the new arrival. Among the many conventions of Greek tragedy this formal pattern seems unobtrusive. In light of the dovetailing of these conventions with what seems to be the fundamental structure of Greek tragedy, we should weigh them carefully in our consideration of the plays.

In this chapter I review and discuss conventions of entrance announcements in Euripides. This will allow us, first, to refine the formulation of the above-stated and related conventions and, second, to explain many of the exceptions to them.[5] When the conventions are not followed, there is usually a solid dramatic reason for it. Finally, we will be able to discuss other conventions and dramatic patterns in Euripides.

1. Announcements Occur only with More than One Person on Stage

Rarely do we find an entrance announcement when only one person is on stage; someone has to be there to hear it.[6] This convention, related to the ones described above, explains the absence of many announcements that those conventions might lead us to expect. For example, Helen does not announce Teukros' entrance at *Hel.* 68 because she is alone on stage. Since the chorus provides a continuous presence of more than one person, there are relatively few examples of an entrance with only one person on stage, and all but one of the other ten occur in the prologue scenes of the plays.[7] There are also six exceptional cases.[8] With at most eleven cases where this convention applies, six exceptions perhaps question its strength. In the following discussion I hope to show that dramatic grounds explain the breaking of the convention in two of the cases and that the other four, all involving gods, form a special group.

Exceptions Involving Mortal Characters

In *Med.*, at the end of her prologue speech, the Nurse, alone on stage, announces the approach of her mistress' children (46–8):

But the children, finished with their games,
Approach, with no thought of their mother's
Woes. For the young mind is not used to pain.

The accompanying Pedagogue, not the announced children, then addresses the Nurse. It is not surprising that the children do not speak; on the tragic stage they do not have speaking roles, only lyric parts in pathetic situations.[9] But why are the children, not the Pedagogue, announced? And why is there an announcement at all with only the Nurse on stage? Because the children are the focus of attention. The Nurse has just finished expressing her fear of Medeia's plotting against the children[10] (the importance of having children is, of course, revealed during the play) and now they appear on stage. The Pedagogue is merely an extension of the children; he exists only because they do. (Note that his reappearance later in the play (894ff) is also only implied.) Furthermore, the announcement picks up the Nurse's fear, as Euripides plays on the ambiguity of *kakôn* ('woes', 48). The children, we are told in the announcement, arrive *mètròs oudèn ennoúmenoi/kakôn* ('with no thought of their mother's woes', 47–8). The phrase *mètròs* ... /*kakôn* can refer both to Medeia's woes (an objective genitive, and this is the more obvious meaning) and to the woes that lie in store for the children *from* Medeia (a subjective genitive). Euripides thus breaks the convention to underscore the importance of the children and Medeia's potential for violence, and he highlights his point with a play on words.

The reason that Elektra announces the approaching chorus at *Or.* 132ff is less clear. (The convention holds for entrances of both actors and chorus.) Does some factor mitigate the anomalous announcement? Perhaps the sleeping Orestes makes the case unexceptional — two persons are on stage.[11] Helen's unannounced entrance earlier in the drama (71) is clearly intended to be surprising, and that might account for the lack of an announcement there.[12] But announcements are made to be heard, and Elektra wants least to disturb her brother's rest. The announcement is precipitated by her deep concern for her half-dead brother; in announcing the chorus she expresses her fear that they will wake him (132–5):[13]

But here come these friends, to share
My lamentations. Maybe they will disturb

> This one's peaceful sleep, and make my eyes
> Melt with tears, when I see my brother mad.

She follows the announcement with an appeal to the chorus that they be quiet lest they wake Orestes.[14] Usually in tragedy the one who arrives on stage begins the dialogue. When this pattern is not followed, often the result is to express the eagerness of the character already on stage.[15] That Elektra atypically announces the approaching chorus and then atypically begins the dialogue highlights her great devotion to her brother (central to the drama's plot and themes) and serves as a prelude to the ensuing lyric duet.

Divine Prologue Scenes

Six times in Euripides' extant plays[16] a divine character speaks the opening lines: *Alk., Hipp., Hek. Tro. Ion, Bakch.* (In *Hek.* the spectre of Polydoros, not a god, delivers the prologue, but it functions in the same way as the others.) In four of these cases (*Alk., Hipp., Hek., Ion*) the divinity, alone on stage, announces an approaching character, the exceptions mentioned above. The special dramatic function that might explain the announcements in *Med.* and *Or.* is not present here. Gods, it seems, can behave differently from mortals in some tragic conventions. Alone on stage, they can make announcements because they are gods.[17] A further look at these six cases amplifies the differences.

Aphrodite announces the approach of Hippolytos and his band (*Hipp.* 51ff); Polydoros' shade announces, then greets his mother (*Hek.* 52ff); and Ion is heralded and 'named' by Hermes (*Ion* 76ff). In all three cases, the divine speaker delivers an opening *rhesis*, announces the oncoming mortal character and departs. The reason given for the departure in each instance is the approaching mortal.[18] The opening of *Bakch.* should be considered along with these three cases, even though it involves a greeting and not an announcement. Dionysos several times in the prologue states that he has changed into mortal form, but even a 'mortal' Dionysos, having called his band of maenads forth (55ff), departs before they arrive. He does not give explicitly their arrival as the reason for his departure, but the pattern is the same as in the other plays: divine prologue speaker, announcement of and/or address to the approaching mortal(s), departure.

The two characters involved in the prologue scene of *Alk.* are both superhuman, and the poet employs a different scheme.

Apollo does not seek to avoid Thanatos, but rather the pollution that will attend Alkestis' death (22–3). (Compare Artemis' words as she leaves Hippolytos in *Hipp.* 1437–9.) He then announces Thanatos, whose opening words (28ff) do nothing to suggest that Apollo has begun to exit. Apollo awaits and converses with him.

Tro. offers the final instance of a divine prologue speaker. Poseidon seems to have made his departing address to Troy ('Goodbye, city that once was fortunate ...,' 45ff) — maybe he has even begun to exit — when Athene appears.[19] Her entrance is surprising. So much so that one critic has suggested that the scene is interpolated.[20] But there is no purpose in excising blameless lines when the dramatic effects are clear. Athene's decision to support the Trojans is a turnabout. What better way to underline this change of heart than with a dramatically unusual and forceful entrance? Secondly, Athene's entrance has not been announced, but it has, in a way, been hinted at: she is mentioned in the final line of Poseidon's adieu (45–7):

But, goodbye city that once was fortunate
And the polished walls. You would still be standing
If Pallas, Zeus' child, had not destroyed you.

Poseidon's mention of his niece 'serves as a link between the end of Poseidon's monologue and Pallas' appearance in the next line.'[21]

Why, we might wonder, do the divinities *not* announce the oncoming mortal characters in *Alk.* and *Tro.* Although *Tro.* presents something of a special situation (discussed in Chapter 5), both cases can be explained along the same lines. Because in *Alk.* and *Tro.*, and only in these two plays, there are two divine characters in the prologue, the scene can conclude with the interactions of the two — the argument of Apollo and Thanatos and the arrangements of Poseidon and Athene. We mentioned above, n. 18, that arrivals of mortals provided *one* motivation for divine exits, explained in the announcements. In the two cases here, other ways of ending the scenes are used.

Gods do not interact with mortals on the Euripidean stage. They can affect and predict the outcome of events, and they can appear on high to make final pronouncements, but only very exceptionally do they participate in the action.[22] In the prologues, after they deliver their *rhesis*, we have seen, they announce or address the oncoming character(s). Divine prologue speakers do not, however, have any contact with new characters unless they also are divine: Apollo can wait for Thanatos and Athene can surprise Poseidon; from mortals, though, they keep their distance. On the other hand, while several times in tragedy one mortal will say to another that one or both of them ought to withdraw because of someone's approach (e.g. *El.* 962ff, *IT* 118ff)[23] nowhere does a mortal alone on stage say that he is getting out of the way because of oncoming character(s).[24] In the only two cases where a mortal makes an announcement to an empty stage, *Med.* 46ff and *Or.* 132ff, we have observed that the character then engages in conversation with the new arrivals.

It has often been remarked that Euripidean prologues are not as dramatically integrated as those of the other two tragedians,[25] and this is especially pronounced in the divine prologue scenes. We have seen the gods' detachment from the action in the practice described above. This detachment is perhaps also suggested by another feature — change of metre.

The divine prologue scenes (except for Thanatos' entering anapests in *Alk.*) are always in iambic trimeter. The following scene, when mortals arrive, always begins in a different metre. The cases of *Alk.* and *Bakch.* are not germane, since the chorus' entry follows and naturally they employ a lyric metre. But strikingly, in the other four instances, where the *parodos* does not follow immediately, we also find metrical variation. In *Tro.* and *Hek.* it is the pathetic anapests of Hekabe; Ion's anapests in *Ion*; and in *Hipp.* the lyrics of Hippolytos and his companions. By comparison, of the four cases in *non*-divine prologue scenes where a second or third character enters to an empty stage (the exact parallel), the metre varies only once — Elektra's song at *El.* 112ff.[26] And here we should point to the anomaly of Elektra having a *second* entrance in this prologue scene.

Change in metre is a basic way to divide a play into smaller units: episodes and odes, and shorter units within episodes. This metrical shift would be appropriate for a mortal's entrance following a divine prologue scene. Assuming that the divinities appeared on stage, and not on high,[27] the change in metre might provide the distance which the *mechane* could provide visually. The evidence on this point is meager, but the suggestion stands.

2. Entrances Immediately after Strophic Songs are not Announced

When Andromache and her child Astyanax enter at *Tro.* 577, immediately after the first stasimon, an announcement heralds their arrival. At *Or.* 356, directly following a strophic song, Menelaos' entrance is announced. Both of these examples contradict the convention outlined above: immediately after a strophic song an entrance is *not* announced. Many other announced entrances also violate this convention. It will be useful and instructive to study these exceptions.

'Moving Tableaux'

What, if anything, do these entrances have in common that might explain the unexpected announcements? Several of them involve the arrival of a chariot, corpse or escorted prisoners, entrances of what Hourmouziades called a 'moving tableau', and, he reasoned, 'therefore some kind of preparation or accompaniment is perfectly justified'.[28] Because of the special nature of such entrances (perhaps extra time was needed for the 'tableau' to enter and take its place in the orchestra), the poet drew special attention to them with the unexpected announcements.

Two 'chariot' entrances in Euripides that occur directly after strophic songs (Andromache's arrival in *Tro.* and Klytaimestra's at *IA* 607[29]) are both preceded by entrance announcements and can be explained on these grounds. Similarly, the impressive (and slow?) arrivals of escorted prisoners would explain the exceptional announcement of Andromache and others at *And.* 501 and the accompanied Orestes and Pylades at *IT* 467; and the solemn movement that might accompany the entrance of a corpse would account for the announcements of Astyanax' corpse (*Tro.* 1123), and the bodies at *Hik.* 798. The special character of two other, comparable entrances is readily observed: the entrance of Alkestis, moribund, with husband and children at *Alk.* 244 and that of the Nurse with the wasting-away Phaidra at *Hipp.* 176 both warrant the exceptional announcements they receive.[30]

Agreement can be found that the preceding cases belong to a special group, but beyond these there is little concurrence,[31] primarily because definitions of a 'moving tableau' have been too narrow, restricted to a certain number of well-defined categories (e.g. chariots, corpses). These basic categories certainly provide the majority of examples, but the concept should be broadened to include any entrance that in some way is slow, solemn or impressive. (Some of the entrances that I will include under this rubric are not, properly speaking, 'tableaux', but I retain the term because most of the examples do belong to one of these categories, and the term is already familiar.) Are we left entirely with subjectivity in determining whether an entrance belongs to these groups? No, the texts, of course, provide clues, and metre is an invaluable guide. As is discussed more fully below, all[32] of the entrances that I would assign to this group are announced in anapestic dimeter and conversely all anapestic dimeter announcements are of these or other special entrances.[33]

Evadne's entrance in *Hik.* is a peculiar scene.[34] The chorus announces her arrival with these anapestic lines (980–9):

> And now I see the holy
> Resting place of Kapaneus
> And outside the temple
> Theseus' funeral offerings to the dead,
> And the famous wife of this man
> Destroyed by thunderbolt, Evadne,
> The daughter of lord Iphis.
> Why, mounting this path,
> Has she climbed the lofty rock,
> Which rises above this house?

Although Kapaneus' funeral procession is mentioned in this announcement, it is never seen on stage.[35] The cliff on which Evadne is thought to be standing overlooks her husband's pyre (1009–11).[36] This off-stage area and the procession must be imagined from the description that is given; it is not seen by the audience. (Compare, e.g., the *teichoskopia* in *Phoin.*) There is no mention of the corpse or attendants.[37] How, in any case, could the arrival of the corpse be so thoroughly ignored in the action that followed? Nowhere in tragedy is there a parallel for such an entrance. The escorting of prisoners or the carrying in of a corpse is an important matter and not to be treated in an off-hand fashion. The reference to the off-stage funeral might contribute to the choice of an anapestic announcement after a strophic song, but it does not totally justify it. Rather, Evadne, entering to her suicide, is like those who enter condemned to death,[38] and thus demands this treatment, especially when the staging (on the roof or some projection behind it) probably required a slow entrance.

Menelaos' entrance at *Or.* 356, preceded by an anapestic announcement and honorific greeting from the chorus, clearly was impressive.[39] The phrase *pollêi habrosúnēi* (349) describes a lordly entrance,[40] and the splendour and pomp of the cowardly Menelaos contrast sharply with the prostrate and squalid Orestes. The twenty-four-line period (356–79) in which the conqueror of Troy tells his tale before he comes into contact with his nephew, lying not very far from him, would be quite in keeping with this impressive entrance.

Also belonging to this category of entrances is the return of Orestes and Pylades from the city (1018), where Orestes and his sister have been condemned to death. Hamilton excludes this entrance, citing Soph. *Ant.* 988 and *Phil.* 730 as parallels.[41] But *are* they parallel? The anapestic announcement at *Or.* 1012–17 reveals how the two arrive:

And here your brother slowly walks,
Condemned to a sentence of death,
With Pylades, the most faithful of all,
Like a brother, guiding
His weakened limbs,
Standing by his side with care.

Pylades is at Orestes' side (*paráseiros*, 1017), caring for him (*kēdosúnōi*, 1017), and guiding his pace (*ithúnōn/noseròn kôlon*, 1015-16). They left the stage with Orestes leaning on Pylades for support (*peribalòn pleuroîs emoîsi pleurà nōchelê nósōi* ('Lean on me, your side worn out by illness against my side', 800, Pylades to Orestes) and they return, we are told, the same way.

The scenes in Sophokles are different. At *Ant.* 988, Teiresias is guided on stage because of his blindness. This is habitual for him, and the poet does not draw attention to his entrance. There is no description of his slow pace, only Teiresias' brief reference to his need for a guide. The scene that at first glance seems to offer a closer parallel is *Phil.* 730, where Philoktetes and Neoptolemos emerge from the cave. The Budé translator, Paul Mazon, for example, writes the following stage direction (p. 36): 'Philoktetes leaves the cave supported by Neoptolemos.' Yet nothing in the text suggests that Philoktetes is supported by Achilleus' son. When they enter the cave, it is Philoktetes who leads in Neoptolemos (674–5), and Neoptolemos' words when they return from the cave do not imply his support of Philoktetes (730–1):

> Come on, if you wish. Why in the world for no reason
> Are you silent and so astounded?

His question to Philoktetes shortly thereafter suggests that he is not in physical contact with him (761):

> Do you want me to take hold of you and touch you?

Physical contact is generally clearly indicated in the texts. Since we lack any such indication here, this entrance, like the one at *Ant.* 988, does not provide a parallel, and *Or.* 1018 is best considered a 'moving tableau'.[42]

Why Talthybios' entrance at *Tro.* 235 warrants an anapestic announcement directly after a strophic song is difficult to see. He is attended by henchmen,[43] but so are many others who receive regular announcements. Perhaps the might and number of the Greeks, making an impressive show, contrasts with the weak position of the Trojan women, an antithesis made explicit later in the drama (726ff). If this is the case, however, we would expect something more to suggest it. This announcement is best considered an exception, not a 'moving tableau'.

Every one of the above cases, except for *Tro.* 235, can be explained as 'moving tableaux', broadly defined — entrances that are in some way slow, solemn or impressive, and announced in anapests. Because of the special quality of these entrances, their announcements directly after strophic songs can be explained and justified.

And all of these announcements, we have noted, are in anapests. The close connection between anapestic announcements and 'moving tableaux' is confirmed in two ways: first, other such entrances — those *not* directly after strophic songs — also receive anapestic announcements, and, secondly, anapestic announcements are used *only* for these entrances and for some divine epiphanies.

The one other chariot arrival, the impressive entrance of Klytaimestra at *El.* 998, a fine contrast to Elektra's squalor emphasised througout the play, is announced in anapests, after the iambic dialogue of Elektra and Orestes. Almost all the entries of corpses receive anapestic announcements: Neoptolemos at *And.* 1173, the fathers' bones carried in by their children at *Hik.* 1123, and Antigone and others leading in the bodies at *Phoin.* 1485. The return at *Hipp.* 1347 of the broken Hippolytos, supported by his companions (see 1358ff and Barrett (ed.), *ad loc.*), is not strictly parallel, but, like Phaidra's first entrance in this play (see above), it functions in the same way as the others. It, too, is announced in anapests.

The exceptions to the tendency to announce the arrival of corpses are either dramatically purposeful or only apparent. When in *Hek.* the servant who has been sent for water to wash Polyxene's corpse returns with the body of Polydoros, she receives no announcement directly after a strophic song. If this entrance were treated like the 'moving tableaux', there should still be an announcement even directly following this song. But Hekabe's discovery of the corpse's identity is much more effective than any announcement could be.[44] Admetos emerges from the *skene* at *Alk.* 606, explaining that his wife is being carried to her burial. No anapestic announcement is found here, because, after the elaborate lamentations over Alkestis in the previous scene, such an announcement is not desired, as this new act focuses on the conflict between Admetos and Pheres. Orestes' and Pylades' arrival with the head of Aigisthos (*El.* 880) and the deluded Agave's with her son's head (*Bakch.* 1168) are quite different from the 'moving tableaux'. Both entrances reveal victors carrying in the slain as their booty, and these jubilant arrivals have nothing in common with the mournful entrances described above.[45] Thus they are not announced in anapests.[46] Shortly after the false triumph of Agave's return to the city, Kadmos enters (1216), followed by servants who carry Pentheus' dismembered corpse. No announcement greets this sad arrival, although the convention 'requires' one, since it does not come directly after a strophic song, and we might very well expect the chorus to herald it in anapests. A possible reason for this exceptional entrance is explored in the next Chapter.

The above-described entrances of corpses are all from the *parodos,* since the catastrophes occurred away from the stage. When corpses are revealed from the *skene* to the spectators, attention is usually called to the entrance, but anapests are not used. Euripides has (probably) four[47] instances. Phaidra's corpse at *Hipp.* 811 is preceded by Theseus' command to open the palace doors (808–10) and is accompanied by lyric lamentations from the chorus, and the appearance of Herakles and his slaughtered family at *Her.* 1031 is announced and accompanied by choral lyrics. At *Hek.* 1049ff Hekabe announces in iambics that Polymestor and the slain children will soon be visible. The chorus at *El.* 1172ff announces in iambics the murderers; the corpses, *if* they are revealed, receive no special notice. If, as is likely, the *ekkyklema* was employed for these appearances of corpses,[48] anapestic announcements, appropriate for the 'moving tableaux' were not, it seems, appropriate for these entrances on the *ekkyklema.*[49]

Several other entrances that we *might* expect to be introduced by anapests are not. On closer examination, we see that they do not warrant anapestic announcements. Herakles' return with Alkestis at *Alk.* 1008, directly following a strophic song, is announced by the chorus in iambic trimeter. Nothing suggests slow or deliberate movement or any other factor that might demand an anapestic announcement. Alkestis may be led in by Herakles, but is she the equivalent of an escorted prisoner?[50] Both the metre and the length (two lines) of the announcement tell against its being considered a 'moving tableau' and receiving an anapestic announcement. It is exceptional because it is announced at all and it will be treated as such in the following section.

In his first appearance in *Bakch.*, Dionysos is the prisoner of Pentheus' servant, but he is not announced directly after a full stasimon. I suggest that the mood and rhythm of the scene do not allow it. The audience knows who the stranger is. Dionysos, though ostensibly Pentheus' prisoner, dominates the scene and the young king with his calm and confidence. The slow entrance of the condemned man, accompanied by an anapestic announcement, would be inappropriate for Dionysos' entrance here. Inappropriate for a different reason, would be a marked entrance for Eurystheus' arrival at *Hkld.* 928. In the cases where anapests announce prisoners, the prisoners are all condemned to an unjust death. The pathos of the scene is created, in part, by the words and form of the announcement. (Note, e.g., the pity of the chorus in the announcements in *And.* and *Her.* and its reservation about Artemis' rites in *IT.*) In *Hkld.*, Eurystheus is presented as the enemy, and is not to be pitied, even if he cannot be put to death. Therefore Euripides does not have a 'moving tableau' entrance for him.[51]

Menelaos arrives with Andromache's son at *And.* 309, threatening to kill him if Andromache will not leave the altar. No special announcement precedes this entrance. Nor should it since this scene is different from those that are so greeted in two respects. First, the infant does not speak in the ensuing dialogue,[52] and, secondly, he is presented more as a 'bargaining chip' than as a prisoner condemned to death. Finally, we should exclude from being considered a 'moving tableau' Orestes' and Pylades' entrance at *IT* 1222. Earlier in the play (a scene discussed above) they entered as escorted prisoners, the latest victims for Artemis' altar. Now, after the joyful recognition of brother and sister, they are part of the plot to deceive Thoas and make their escape. Note that these characters, like Andromache's infant in *And.*, do not speak in the scene. Although they are bound and under guard (see 1204ff), they are ostensibly part of a religious procession, and in fact part of the deception of Thoas. They are announced (as expected in the middle of the act[53]) in iambic trimeter, but no special attention is drawn to their entrance. They take no verbal part in the scene and they depart almost as soon as they enter (1222/1233).

The second confirmation of the close tie between 'moving tableaux' and anapestic announcements is that anapests are not used to announce other types of entrances. The anapests at *Ion* 1244ff do not announce Kreousa (see the discussion below in Section 3). Talthybios' entrance at *Tro.* 1260 (also considered in Section 3) is not preceded by an announcement. The only other two[54] entrances that are announced in anapests are both of divine appearances. The final section of this Chapter is devoted to a consideration of divine epiphanies outside of the prologue scenes.

It might appear that the discussion on 'moving tableaux' involves circular reasoning: anapests announce 'moving tableaux' and 'moving tableaux' are defined by anapestic announcements. This is not the case. Both the action, as implied in the text, and the metre of the announcement together define a 'moving tableau'; one factor informs the other. The cases that find easy agreement are all announced in anapests, suggesting that the metrical element might be a factor in determining what constitutes a 'tableau'. Attempts to define 'moving tableaux' by overly precise categories are ultimately unsatisfactory because of the problems of definition and assignment and, more important, because such attempts do not get at the crux of the issue. The entrance of a corpse or prisoner does not receive special treatment *because of* the corpse or prisoner. Otherwise all such entrances would be so handled. Rather the way in which these entrances are made determines how they are treated. As stated earlier, entrances that are in some way slow, solemn, or impressive (and this includes many of the entrances involving corpses, chariots and prisoners) will be announced even directly after a strophic song, and in anapestic dimeter. The metrical form matches the entrance. A final argument for the validity of our general definition: exceptions do exist. Although there are no cases of what I would call a 'moving tableau' that are not announced in anapestic dimeter, there are at least two entrances (*Tro.* 235 and *Hypsipyle* fr. 1 iv l.15) announced in anapests where the reason for such an announcement is not evident.

By this definition, then, there are twelve cases in the extant plays where an entrance directly after a strophic song is announced because the entrance involves a 'moving tableau': ≈ *Alk.* 244, *Hipp.* 176, *And.* 501, *Hik.* 798, 990, *Her.* 451, *Tro.* 577, 1123, *IT* 467, *Or.* 356, 1018, *IA* 607. The special nature of these entrances justifies the breaking of the entrance convention.

Other Exceptions

Other exceptions, however, do exist. Two have already been discussed: Herakles' return with Alkestis at *Alk.* 1008 and Talthybios' entrance at *Tro.* 235. The messenger who enters at *Hipp.* 1153 is announced by the chorus immediately after a strophic song. Lykos at *Her.* 140 is announced under the same conditions. Problems attend Kreon's entrance at *Phoin.* 1310. He does not carry a corpse, but whether Euripides wrote this scene or not remains unclear.[55] In addition to other peculiarities, we should observe that the announcement of Kreon at 1308–9 in trochaic tetrameter is the only example in Euripides of an announcemment in this metre without preceding or following tetrameters.[56] At the very least, it is a curious passage and best remembered as such.

Why in these instances did the playwright go against the convention of having no announcement for an entrance directly after a strophic song, at which juncture the audience expected an arrival? Do these cases share common characteristics? All five entrances are from the *parodos*, but in general the same conventions apply to entrances from the *skene* and *parodos*. The announcements are all very typical in language; no clue lies here. The type of person announced provides no common link (Herakles, two rulers, messenger and herald).

For three of these cases there is a possible shared explanation. In *Alk.*, *Her.* and *Tro.* a structural peculiarity may account for the announcements: there is no exit prior to the strophic song. According to Taplin's thesis for the basic structure of the tragedies, act-dividing songs are preceded by exits and followed by entrances. The pattern allows many variations, but when it is diverged from, we must pay close attention to the purpose and result of the variation.

Almost always an exit precedes a strophic song, either immediately or shortly before.[57] Four times, however, no one exits before an uninterrupted strophic song which is followed immediately by an entrance.[58] Three of these instances occur before the strophic songs that are followed by the exceptional announced entrances at *Alk.*, *Her.* and *Tro.* The fourth is found in *Hik.*, where no exit precedes the parodos and Theseus arrives immediately after the song, unannounced. This case might seem to weaken the suggestion that the lack of an exit before a strophic song makes necessary the announcement of an immediately following entrance, but it has, I think, an explanation. Aithra informs us at the end of her opening *rhesis* that she has sent for Theseus (36–7). He is not announced *because* he has been sent for — an 'Ersatz' announcement.[59] To object that this is not an 'Ersatz' announcement because the ode intervenes, breaking up the temporal continuity, is not compelling.[60] In our present case an actor remains on stage during the song, in which situation the time that elapses during the song is never very long, since the presence of the actor provides that continuity from one act to the next.[61]

A break in the basic structure, then, perhaps accounts for apparent breaks in the conventions of entrance announcements. Herakles in *Alk.*, Lykos in *Her.* and Talthybios in *Tro.* are announced directly after a strophic song because no exit preceded the song. Without that exit, the demarcation between the acts was diminished and the entrance after the song was felt to occur within the act, not at the beginning of one, thus necessitating an announcement. The structure in *Alk.* is additionally peculiar: after the return of the chorus and Admetos, there is a one-actor scene, with no exit before the next song. That the announcement of Talthybios in *Tro.* is in anapests remains puzzling.[62]

Of the remaining two exceptions, the peculiarities of *Phoin.*

1310 have been mentioned. For the anomalous announced entrance of the messenger at *Hipp.* 1153 I offer a tentative suggestion. The problems surrounding the preceding lyric (1102–50) are well-known: why the confusion of genders? is there a subsidiary chorus? If there is a subsidiary chorus (Barrett (ed.), *ad loc.*, does not argue persuasively that there is not), could they not leave the stage at the end of the second strophe, after singing strophes a and b, where the masculine participles are found?[63] The unusual departure within, not before, the lyric would then account for the unusual announcement of the messenger at the start of the next scene.

3. Entrances Not Directly After Strophic Songs Are Announced

Immediately after a strophic song, an entrance is not announced, unless the nature of the entrance ('moving tableau') or a structural break demands it. Hamilton, in his chief contribution to the study of entrance announcements, noticed that the converse of this convention was also true: an entrance not directly following a strophic song[64] is announced. One restriction, of course, is that more than one person must be on stage; someone has to hear the announcement (see Section 1 above).

Even with this proviso, many[65] apparently genuine exceptions remain — i.e., unannounced entrances not directly after a strophic lyric when more than one person is on stage. Of these, some are clearly intended to be surprising: the priestess in *Ion*, the servant in *Hel.*, Makaria in *Hkld.*, and the old man in *IA* all enter suddenly to turn about the course of events. (The entry of the messenger at *IA* 414 certainly surprises, but this scene is of dubious authenticity.[66] Although not all surprise entrances are unannounced, surprise seems to be one reason for the lack of an announcement.[67] (Surprise entrances without and with announcements are considered in Chapter 3.) The remaining exceptions are considered here.

Excluded from discussion are entrances with 'Ersatz' announcements, i.e., when, after noise is heard from within, someone enters from the *skene* (e.g. Hekabe at *Hek.* 1044), or someone is summoned (e.g. Elektra at *El.* 751) or responds to a cry for help or of distress (e.g. the chorus at *Hkld.* 73).[68] These are not exceptions. Theseus' entrance at *Hipp.* 790 belongs to this last group.[69] He enters immediately after the Nurse has discovered and the chorus learned of Phaidra's hanged body. The Nurse's first words upon making this discovery issue a cry for help (776): *ioù ioú, boēdromeîte pántes hoi pélas dómōn* ('Respond to my cry, everyone who's near the house'). And Theseus' opening words, like the chorus' in *Hkld.*, reveal that he has heard the cry (790–3):[70]

Women, do you know what cry came from the house?
For the house does not think to open the gates
And to give me, returned from the oracle, a friendly greeting.

We should also consider that in their agitation and hesitation ('What are we to do?', 782) before Theseus arrives, the chorus' movement has perhaps precluded their noticing his arrival. This seems to be the implication of his opening remarks.

When Theseus makes his final entrance in *Hik.* is uncertain. The subsidiary chorus goes off with Adrastos and Theseus at 954, and it would be highly unusual for the children's chorus to re-enter independently, since secondary characters stay with the person to whom they are attached. They can take the spotlight, as it were, but they function with, not without, their primary characters. Before their exit in *Hik.* the children do not act independently, nor is there reason to think they do afterwards. We should simply imagine that the chilren's chorus enters, followed in by Adrastos and Theseus.[71] If Theseus enters at 1123, his unannounced arrival, directly after a strophic song, is unexceptional. Earlier in the play, however, when Theseus was silent during the lamentations of Adrastos and the chorus, his first words explained his silence (838–40).

The chorus in *Ion* follows a brief lyric with these anapests (1244–9):

Escape is impossible,
Unless a god desires to whisk us away.
What, poor mistress, remains
For your spirit to suffer?
We wanted to hurt those near to us —
Will *we* now suffer justly?

Do these words address the on-rushing Kreousa? Or are they an apostrophe? Kreousa, it is evident from the following action, does not hear these words, in contrast to the similar situation at Soph. *Ant.* 379–85, where contact is made between the chorus and the guard leading in Antigone.[72] These words do not address Kreousa or announce her arrival, but they do serve as a link to her entrance. (This will be discussed in Chapter 3.)

Talthybios' return at *Tro.* 1260 is not heralded. Directly before he enters, the chorus in lyric anapests cries out at the torches it spots on the acropolis (1256–9):

> Look! What fiery hands do I see
> Waving torches on the heights of Ilion?
> Some new woe
> Is at hand for Troy.

As soon as he arrives, Talthybios orders henchmen to put these torches to the city. The action takes place off-stage, and the audience is asked to visualise it,[73] as they are asked to imagine the scene described in *Phoin.*'s *teichoskopia* or Kapaneus' pyre in *Hik.* Just as cries can be heard by someone off-stage, orders can be given to those beyond the audience's vision. The emphasis in the words precediɪg the entrance falls not on the Greeks' lackey but on the flames that will demolish Troy, the destruction ordered in the herald's first words. These words of the chorus reinforce the importance of the fire: the adjective *phlogéas* ('fiery') is transferred to *chéras* ('hands'), emphasising 'the fact that the women were struck by the sight of the flames and that the men were noticed only because of the torches which they carried.'[74] The torch plays a key thematic role in the whole Trojan trilogy.[75]

The messenger who reports Orestes' victory over Aigisthos in *El.* informs Electra that her brother will soon appear carrying the head of his victim (855–7). This 'announcement in advance' has many parallels.[76] Such 'announcements in advance', however, do not alter the convention that an entrance not directly after a strophic song is announced. But it should be noted that most of these involve a 'moving tableau' and would receive an announcement in any case. The messenger's advance notice, then, does not explain the lack of an announcement. Nor should Elektra's greeting be equated with an announcement. Greetings to a character as he enters are not very common, since the arriving character usually initiates the dialogue,[77] and often they follow an announcement made by the same or a different person (e.g. *Hkld.* 48ff and *Or.* 1013ff). Why, then, are Orestes and Pylades not announced? That Elektra speaks first when they enter suggests the answer. We have already observed that this uncommon practice expresses the special eagerness, concern etc. of the person on stage who speaks first. Elektra's joy and congratulations at the death of Aigisthos are given greater expression with this presentation. Maybe the 'announcement in advance' combined with the atypical address from Elektra weakened the need for a formal announcement.

Helen's unannounced entrance after consulting Theonoe in *Hel.* deserves special consideration, as the chorus' exit with her and the following 'epiparodos' create an unusual structure. A comparison with the other 'epiparodoi' in Greek tragedy is instructive.[78] In Soph. *Ai.* 814/866ff it is important that Tekmessa discover the body herself. Thus she enters independent of and after the chorus.[79] In Aisch. *Eum.* 231/244ff it is clear that Orestes re-enters before the pursuing Furies. When Admetos returns from burying his wife in *Alk.*, there is no suggestion that the chorus enters separately; they exit and re-enter together. The text of *Hel.* suggests the same pattern: the independence of actor and chorus that we find in *Ai.* and *Eum.* is neither hinted at nor desired. Helen exits with the chorus into the *skene*, and, it seems, she follows them out as they sing a brief astrophic song, remaining silent until 528.[80]

When does the newly outfitted Menelaos enter later in *Hel.* — at 1369 with his wife or at 1390 with Theoklymenos? If the former, no announcement is needed; if the latter, one would normally be expected. We cannot be certain, but the evidence points to an entrance with the king. If he does enter with Helen, her treatment of him is quite peculiar: she refers to him exclusively in the third person and uses no deictic pronoun or other means of alluding to his presence. It is rather odd 'if he has to be dumbly present while Helen points out at some length his improved appearance, his clean clothes, his armour, and his high hopes.'[81] An arrival with Theoklymenos[82] explains away these peculiarities, but creates another one: why is he not announced? Menelaos in this scene is a subordinate character, under the king's auspices. The scene focuses on Helen in her final deception of Theoklymenos; Menelaos speaks only after he has been addressed directly and (probably) after the king's departure. We have seen many examples in Euripides where an announcement excludes someone with a speaking part and highlights another of the entrants. Here, however, both of the entrants, the one announced and the one unannounced, have speaking parts.

The messenger's unannounced arrival at *IA* 1532 is exceptional, if the passage is genuine. Page has made a strong case against its authenticity,[83] but it is worth remembering that in almost every tradition of the story Artemis rescues Iphigeneia.[84] If Euripides wrote an ending to this play, it most probably contained some account of this reversal of fortune, maybe marked by a surprise entrance.

Exceptionally, neither Amphitryon nor Megara announces the chorus' entrance at *Her.* 107. It is interesting that only rarely is a choral entrance announced by someone who then remains on stage; the tendency is to clear the stage before the chorus arrives, unless suppliants (who obviously must remain) are present or a single actor stays. But all the other instances of no announcement for the chorus can be explained on the principle of the number of persons on stage. A possible reason for this break in the convention is considered in Chapter 5.

Divine Epiphanies Beyond the Prologue

Many questions surround the *mechane* and its use in divine epiphanies.[85] My purpose here is not to enter into that fray, but to comment briefly on the connection between these appearances and entrance announcements.

Dignus vindice nodus. Sometimes this is the reason for a divine appearance near the end of the play, but often there is no knot to be cut, only loose ends to be picked up. Euripides has fourteen instances of a divine appearance beyond the prologue: *Med.* 1317,[86] *Hipp.* 1283, *And.* 1231, *Hik.* 1183, *Her.* 822, *Ion* 1553, *El.* 1238, *IT* 1435, *Hel.* 1642, *Or.* 1625, *Bakch.*, *Hypsipyle* fr. 64 iii,[87] *Antiope* fr. 48 l. 67 (Kambitsis), *Erechtheus* fr. 65 l. 55 (Austin). Deciding which of these required a cutting of the knot allows for some subjectivity, but I think that there can be little doubt about four of them.

In *Hel.*, when Theoklymenos is about to punish his sister and human intervention is not sufficient, the Dioskouroi bring him to a halt with these words as they appear (1642–3):

Check[88] your rage, which drives you off course,
Theoklymenos, lord of this land.

Similarly, in *Or.* Orestes' threat to murder Hermione and the responding battle cry from Menelaos are met with divine interdiction, as Apollo appears, commanding (1625):

Menelaos, stop your whetted anger.

Hermes arrives in like fashion to interrupt Amphion's murder of Lykos in *Antiope* (fr. 48 ll. 67–8):

Stop your murderous charge, lord Amphion,
I command you.

In the fourth situation the danger to be averted is not as immediate as in the other three cases and the language is not so abrupt, but it seems very much like the others. In *IT* Athene stops Thoas, who has threatened the chorus and is about to muster forces against Orestes, with these words (1435–6):

How far, lord Thoas, are you carrying this prosecution?
Listen to what I, Athene, have to say.

None of the other epiphanies occurs at such a crisis. In these plays a god appears to 'set things straight' and/or to explain a future cult, but none resolves a pressing conflict.

In the four plays where the gods interrupt a violent action, they are not announced;[89] in the other cases, sometimes they are and sometimes they are not. Twice anapestic announcements herald the divine entrance (Thetis in *And.* and the Dioskouroi in *El.*). Anapests are elsewhere used for entrances that are in some way slow, solemn or impressive. A divine appearance, especially from the *mechane*, would qualify as such an entrance, but we must note that not all divine entrances are so marked.[90] The sudden and shocking appearance of Iris and Lyssa in *Her.* receives an excited lyric announcement from the chorus. Only once does an actor announce the divinity — Ion's announcement of Athene in iambic trimeter in *Ion.* (Athene's entrance to stop Ion from approaching Apollo's temple to question the god on embarrassing matters does have some similarity to the four that stop violent action, but the

god's language upon entrance and the action stopped are significantly different.)

Only this last entrance, Athene's in *Ion*, and the same goddess'
entrance in *Erechtheus*,[91] conform to the conventions of entrance
announcements and strophic songs. Three are announced directly
after strophic songs (the anapests in two of these cases might, as
suggested above, be appropriate) and of the nine not following
such lyrics, all but two are unannounced.

In a sense, all divine appearances are surprises; neither the
character nor the audience is prepared for them (although an
experienced member of the audience might expect them now and
then). Of course, not all surprising entrances are unannounced; so
the announcements in a few of these cases need not lessen the surprise. We can conclude only this: when the god interrupts a violent
action, the appearance is unannounced, since an announcement
would be inappropriate to the sudden intervention; when the
entrance does not occur at such a crisis, sometimes there is an
announcement, and sometimes not. We might also observe that in
the announcements never is the divinity named; a supernatural
presence is merely referred to. If, as seems likely, the divinities
appeared from the *mechane*, possibly a technical reason prevented
recognition, but realism was not an overriding concern of the
Greek stage. Maybe mortals should not be expected to recognise
gods, but again, it seems, the distance between mortals and
immortals is suggested.

Notes

1. See Hamilton, 63–7, for a concise statement and thorough rebuttal of these
theories, with the relevant bibliography.

2. Hamilton, 67–8, shows that P. Graeber, *De poetarum Atticorum arte
scaenica quaestiones quinque* (Diss. Göttingen 1911) and Hourmouziades are
wrong in maintaining this. In general the same conventions obtain for entrances
from the *skene* and the *parodos*. See, e.g., Mastronarde, 26–30.

3. Hourmouziades, in addition to offering insightful remarks on several other
topics, made some very important observations about entrance announcements
(137–45). It was Hamilton, however, who corrected, modified and expanded
several of them. Here, Hourmouziades first observed the convention in a different
and less precise formulation and Hamilton, 68–71, modified it and noticed that
the converse is also true. I have stated the convention with a further modification
of my own — 'uninterrupted strophic song' for 'strophic chorus'. For a discussion
of this change, see the Appendix. There are further restrictions on these
conventions and, of course, other conventions, which will be discussed in this
chapter.

4. Taplin, esp. 49–60, and earlier in 'Aeschylean Silences and Silences in Aeschylus', *HSCP* 76 (1972), 84. Hamilton also saw the implications of these conventions.

5. For example, according to Hamilton's figures, 71, the above-stated convention is followed by Aischylos, Sophokles, and Euripides seventy-two eighty, and eighty-eight per cent of the time, respectively. Some of these he readily explains; others can be explained with further discussion. I trust that it is clear that I do not mean to criticise Hamilton. He obviously did not have the space for discussion of the individual cases and did not intend to present reasons for all of the exceptions.

6. Hamilton, 67–8, observes this, again following up a less precise statement of Hourmouziades.

7. The cases of an unheralded announcement with only one person on stage are: *Alk.* 773, *Med.* 131, *And.* 56, 117, *Hek.* 98, *Ion* 184, *Tro.* 48, *El.* 54, *Hel.* 68 (mentioned above), 179, and *Or.* 71. (The servant is alone on stage when Herakles enters at *Alk.* 773 because the chorus has left to attend Alkestis' burial.) I will suggest later in this chapter that other factors could account for the lack of announcement at *Tro.* 48.

8. Of these six, Hamilton, 68 and 81 note c, queries *Med.* 49, since he considers unannounced, 'a character who enters in a group that is announced and who himself is not specifically designated as part of that group.'

9. They do have speaking parts from within, however. For children on the stage, see A.M. Dale (ed.), *Alcestis* (Oxford 1954) xix-xx, and G.M. Sikakis, 'Children in Greek Tragedy', *BICS* 26 (1979), 67–80.

10. The announcement follows the expression of this fear even more closely if we agree, as does D.L. Page (ed.), with Dindorf's excision of 38–43.

11. In *Hkld.*, e.g., Iolaos announces the herald (48–51) because the children, albeit mute, are present; in fact, he makes the announcement by way of explaining to the children the command that they hold on to his robe.

12. Although not all unannounced entrances are meant to be surprising, surprise can be a reason for the lack of an announcement, as we will later discuss in Chapter 3.

13. A similar scene, not involving entrance announcements, of someone afraid that noise will wake a sleeping character and demanding silence is found in *Her.* 1042ff.

14. I agree with Biehl (ed.) in not following Wilamowitz' excision of this four-line address.

15. For some examples, see Taplin, 397, and Mastronarde, 22 n. 16.

16. Among the fragments, it seems that Artemis delivered the prologue in *Meleagros* and Poseidon or Athene in *Erechtheus*.

17. Hamilton, 68, also explains these exceptions on the grounds of the speakers' divinity, and remarks that 'the natural conclusion is that the god in each case is speaking to the audience'. D. Bain, 'Audience Address in Greek Tragedy', *CQ* n.s. 25 (1975), 13–25, is the best recent treatment of the problems involved in audience address in Greek tragedy.

18. Hourmouziades, 157, apropos of the parting lines of Aphrodite in *Hipp.* and Hermes in *Ion*, remarks, 'the values seem to have been reversed: the departure of the gods is a pretext for the introduction not vice versa; conventional though the formula [*allá.* ... *gár*] may have been, neither of the gods could introduce a new character without giving a reason for doing so, especially as no other is present.' The conventional formula is *not* used in *Ion*: *allá* and *gár* are independent (see *Greek Particles*[2], 8). Nor does Polydoros' ghost employ it in *Hek.* More important, the gods do not have to introduce the new characters. Entrance announcements provided *one* way (a convenient one) of motivating the exit. Euripides chose this

way of making the transition from one scene to the next.

19. Hamilton, 70, simply treats this as an unexceptional case of no announcement with only one person on stage. This entrance is also discussed in Chapters 3 and 5.

20. J.R. Wilson, 'An Interpolation in the Prologue of Euripides' *Troades*', *GRBS* 8 (1967), 205–23.

21. So described by K.H. Lee (ed.), *Troades, ad loc.*

22. The 'mortal' Dionysos in *Bakch.* presents a unique case. The divine intervention in the middle of *Her.* has much in common with final epiphanies.

23. See Taplin, 334–5, for the examples in Aischylos and Sophokles. New Comedy has several examples of the chorus being introduced by a getting-out-of-the-way character; see E.W. Handley, *The Dyskolos of Menander* (Cambridge, Mass. 1965), 171–2.

24. A possible instance might be *Alope* fr. 105 N². The Nurse, the probable speaker of these lines, perhaps leaves in modesty before the approaching athletes, but we do not know whether or not anyone else is present. The nearest example in the extant plays is Menelaos' exit at *Hel.* 514, where he goes into hiding in fear of Theoklymenos (cf. 505ff). He makes no announcement or greeting, however, and the chorus and Helen next appear on stage; Theoklymenos does not enter for another 600 lines.

25. This is not the place to survey the function of Euripidean prologues, but let me make it clear that I do not think that they are without importance or artful design. Although other characters do not respond to the divine prologues, the audience does, and the prologues help to create the backdrop for the action and the themes of the dramas. On the characteristics of Euripidean prologues, see W. Nestle, *Die Struktur des Eingangs in der attischen Tragödie* (Stuttgart 1930).

26. The other cases are Orestes' and Pylades' entrances at *El.* 82 and *IT* 67 and the entrance of Antigone and the Pedagogue at *Phoin* 88. As implied in the text, additional entrances to a stage already occupied should not be included. (Those entrances, if included, would strengthen my claim.) Amphion's first entrance in *Antiope* might offer another example of metrical variation upon entrance in a non-divine prologue scene, but too much of this play's opening is uncertain. See J. Kambitsis (ed.), *L'Antiope d'Euripide* (Athens 1972), xii–xiii.

27. Nothing in any of the texts suggests otherwise. See, e.g., Hormouziades' discussion of the evidence, 156–63.

28. Hamilton accepted the principle and the term 'moving tableau', but objected to what he felt was its somewhat imprecise use.

29. I think that Euripides wrote something akin to the entrance announcement that the mss. present (598–606). For the textual problems of this passage, see D.L. Page, *Actors' Interpolations in Greek Tragedy* (Oxford 1934), 160-1.

30. Hamilton, 68 n. 18, explains that he adds these two to the instances of 'dead body tableaux'. How precisely these scenes were first staged is uncertain. In both plays, however, the texts suggest that a bed/couch was brought in and employed in some way, perhaps to carry in the weakened heroines (likely, I think, for Phaidra, less so for Alkestis). This would add to the processional quality of the entrances.

31. For example, Hourmouziades and Hamilton agree on only seven cases: five of those discussed above (not *IA* 607, presumably an oversight by Hourmouziades, as is his neglect of *Alk.* 244, and *Hipp.* 176), Evadne's entrance at *Hik.* 990 and that of Herakles' family, condemned to death, at *Her.* 451. This last entrance both Hourmouziades and Hamilton categorise as an entrance of escorted prisoners, but they must enter unaccompanied, as is clear from Herakles' arrival later. However, we classify this entrance ('escorted prisoners' or 'persons condemned to death'), it unquestionably is a 'moving tableau'.

32. Actually the entrance at *Alk.* 244 is announced at the end of the choral

lyric; anapests then follow, which comment on the pain marriage can bring, as seen in the case now presented to the audience.

33. Taplin, 73, treats the issue only in passing, but he correctly observes the connection between the anapests and this type of entrance. He also implicitly (he does not refer to 'moving tableaux') opts for a broad definition: 'In nearly every case [of an anapestic announcement] there is some obvious way in which the entry is slow or stately'. Hourmouziades, 144, in a more limited context, also mentions the link between anapestic announcements and some of these entrances.

34. At least two scholars have declared it interpolated: G. Norwood, *Essays on Euripidean Drama* (London 1954), esp. 159–60, and P. Arnott, *Greek Scenic Conventions in the fifth century B.C.* (Oxford 1962), 137-8.

35. As supposed by Hamilton, 68 n. 18.

36. The staging of the scene is uncertain. With Collard (ed.), vol. I, 15–16, I am against the *mechane* and favour the roof or some projection behind it. See also Hourmouziades, 32–33, and for other suggestions Collard, esp. 16 n. 61.

37. The deictic *Fasd(e)* (980) is not germane, the chorus (and Evadne) 'sees' the off-stage area, even though the audience does not. For more on tragic *hóde*, see D. Bain, 'The Prologue of Euripides' *Iphigenie in Aulis*', *CQ* n.s. 27 (1977), 25.

38. A similar emotional response from the audience is sought here and in those cases. Both Hamilton and Hourmouziades consider it a 'moving tableau', but the former, as indicated in n. 35 above, incorrectly thought the arrival of a corpse caused the announcement. My view corresponds to Hourmouziades', who believes, 141, that it was the combination of 'the funeral procession off-stage and Evadne's impressive appearance on the rock' that demanded this attention.

39. Neither Hourmouziades nor Hamilton considers it a 'moving tableau'; Taplin, 73, lists it among entries that are 'grand or pompous'. See the remarks of W. Bichl (ed.), *ad loc.*

40. The reading and meaning of the phrase are disputed. See Wecklein, Paley, Di Benedetto, and Biehl (eds.). I follow Murray's text. Whether the phrase refers to Menelaos' gait or his garments, he is described as arriving in an impressive manner.

41. Hamilton, 69 n. 21.

42. Hourmouziades treats it as such, as does (implicitly) Taplin.

43. Presumably more than one, as elsewhere in the play. The singular imperative *ánoige* (304) need not show that only one attendant is present.

44. Hamilton makes the same point, 68 n. 18.

45. Hamilton lists them among 'dead body tableaux'.

46. Agave is announced in iambic trimeters; Orestes and Pylades are greeted, not announced.

47. Medeia's entrance in the chariot with the bodies of the slain children (which are not visible to the audience) at the finale of *Med.* is obviously not included here. It is discussed in Chapter 3.

48. On the use of the *ekkyklema* for these scenes, see esp. Hourmouziades, 98ff. In general on this device, see the bibliography in Taplin, 442–3.

49. The evidence is very slight; I do not wish to overstate the observation.

50. As Hamilton claims, 68 n. 18.

51. Helen's entrance at *Tro.* 895 is also not a 'moving tableau'. As is the case for Eurystheus in *Hkld.*, it would be inappropriate for Helen to have an affecting entrance here. Nor is a regular announcement needed, because Menelaos has sent attendants to bring her forth — she has an 'Ersatz' announcement. This term, coined by Nestle, above n. 25 (Hamilton adopted the concept and used the term 'doubtful' to describe the same types of entrances), refers to those cases where someone has been sent for or called forth, or a noise (often of the *skene* door) has preceded the entrance. These entrances, even when they occur in the middle of an

act, do not need an announcement, because the audience has reason to expect them. See Hamilton, 71, on the ways in which these 'Ersatz' announcements function as ordinary announcements do.

52. Hamilton, 68 n. 18, also mentions this as a mitigating factor.

53. They have been sent for, so an announcement of any sort is not strictly needed. But since they do not take part in the dialogue, the announcement marks their arrival.

54. In the fragments there are least three others. At *Phaethon* 102ff (Diggle), after a strophic choral song, the chorus announces Merops, the herald and Phaethon as they emerge from the *skene*. This is the only unqualified simultaneous triple entrance in tragedy, and both the odd phrase *triploûn zeûgos* (104) and the anapestic announcement underline the unusual nature of the entrance (see Taplin, 241). In the *Phrixos* (*POxy* 2685 fr. i ll 10ff.) the carrying out of Ino's dowry seems quite clearly to be announced in these anapests (see *POxy* vol. 34, 8–13, and Taplin, 73 n. 4). The reason for the anapests is not clear; perhaps the 'defiant stand' (Taplin) that Ino is making here involves an impressive display of her dowry. We cannot tell whether the lyrics that precede this announcement are strophic or not. After the *parodos* of *Hypsipyle* (fr. 1 iv) Amphiaraos is announced. According to Bond's (ed.) analysis of the *parodos*, the lyric is strophic. No reason for this announcement is apparent; it must be considered exceptional.

55. On the problems of this scene, see E. Fraenkel, 'Zu den Phoenissen des Euripides', *SBAW* (1963), 71–86, H. Diller (rev.), *Gnomon* 36 (1964), 641–50, and H. Erbse, 'Beiträge zum Verständnis der euripideischen 'Phoinissen'', *Philologus* 110 (1966), 15–19.

56. In Euripides there are at least six other examples of announcements in trochaic tetrameter, all in the context of this metre: *Ion* 514–16, 1257–8, *IT* 1222–5, ≈ *Or.* 1549–50, *Bakch.* 638–9, *IA* 1338–9.

57. There are a few examples in Euripides of a rather lengthy interval between the exit and the song where, 'the tailpiece is longer and forms a kind of independent scene' (Taplin, 110). But the situation in *Tro.* is not analogous to these, since, although the gods depart at 97, Hekabe's laments are not a tailpiece to the earlier scene: she does not 'enter' until after they leave.

58. There is no exit before the *parodos* in *Hkld.*, *Hek.*, and *Ion.* But these cases are not relevant to our discussion, since the songs in *Hek.* and *Ion* are not uninterrupted, and therefore the following entrances are announced, and after the *parodos* of *Hkld.* there are spoken iambics before the announced arrival of Demophon and Akamas. Spoken iambics also intervene between the *parodos* and the announcement of Orestes and Pylades at *El.* 215ff.

59. See above, n. 51.

60. This is Hamilton's (81 note c) reason for not considering it one.

61. See Graeber, above n. 2, 45. On the issue of temporal continuity, see J. de Romilly, *Time in Greek Tragedy* (Ithaca, N. Y. 1968) *passim* and Taplin, 290–4.

62. As does the announcement in *Hypsipyle*, fr. 1 iv 11, 10ff.

63. The suggestion, made originally by Verrall (ed., Aische. *Ag.*, l) that a subsidiary male chorus sings the two strophes has found many supporters; see recently G. Bond, *Hermathena* 129 (1980) 59–63.

64. Hamilton, as mentioned above n. 3, states the convention with the phrase 'strophic chorus,' not 'strophic lyric' (see the Appendix).

65. Hamilton cites fourteen. They differ from our examples in the exclusion of *Or* 1567 and *IA* 855, which he considers to have 'Ersatz' announcements, and the inclusion of *Hipp.* 790 and *IA* 819. The first two do *not* in my view have 'Ersatz' announcements, and they are discussed in Chapter Three. *Hipp.* 790 does have an 'Ersatz' announcement, as described below. *IA* 819, like the first two, is treated in the next Chapter.

66. See Page, above n. 29, 151ff. Murray (ed.) thinks it is authentic; England (ed.), Nauck (ed.) and Prinz-Wecklein (eds.) are among those who delete the scene.

67. The same principle, agreed to also by Hamilton, explains several unannounced entrances in Aischylos and Sophokles, for which see Hamilton, 70-1.

68. See above, n. 51.

69. Taplin lists it among his examples, while Hamilton thinks the lack of an announcement is exceptional (see above n. 65).

70. For the problems of the text and the interpretation suggested in this translation, see Barrett (ed.), *ad loc.*

71. Bodensteiner and the editors of the Budé text also propose this staging; Hamilton thinks that it is possible. For more on the staging of the scene, see J. Carrière, *Le choeur secondaire dans le drame grec, sur une ressource méconnue de la scène antique* (Paris 1977), 51-9.

72. This is Mastronarde's argument, 94 and n. 51.

73. Lee (ed.), *Troades, ad loc.*, correctly defends this staging against Arnott's proposal, above n. 34, p. 100, that this scene shifts, and now the *skene* represents the walls of Troy.

74. Lee (ed.), *ad loc.*

75. See recently, R. Scodel, *The Trojan Trilogy of Euripides* Hypomnemata 60 (Göttingen 1980), 76-8.

76. See C. Harms, *De introitu personarum in Euripide et novae comoediae fabulis* (Diss. Göttingen 1914), 49ff.

77. See n. 15 above.

78. *Rhes.* 564/674ff is not considered here because it involves only the chorus. *Phaethon* does not have an 'epiparodos'; see Diggle (ed.), 150.

79. Jebb, Stanford, and Kamerbeek in their commentaries all agree that she is not visible until 891 or 894.

80. Bodensteiner, and Kannicht (ed.) place her entrance at 528; Dale (ed.) says merely, 'The Chorus re-enters first.'; and Hamilton in his appendix questions 528 for the entrance. Taplin, 194 n. 3, prefers 528, but admits an earlier entrance with the chorus is possible.

81. Dale (ed.), *ad loc.* Although odd, such a scene is certainly conceivable from Euripides.

82. Kannicht and Campbell are among the editors who favour an entrance here; Wecklein dissents. Theoklymenos refers to Menelaos as *ho xénos* ('the foreigner', 1390) when he enters, but this need not imply that Menelaos enters with him.

83. Page, above n. 29, 192-9.

84. For Euripides' treatment in this play of the Iphigeneia legend, see F. Jouan, *Euripide et les légendes des chants cypriens* (Paris 1966), 274-92.

85. The issues remain unresolved. See, e.g., Barrett (ed.), *Hipp.*, 396-6, Hourmouziades, 146-69, and Talin, 443-7. The fullest treatments of these divine appearances in Euripides are: A. Spira, *Untersuchungen zum Deus ex machina bei Sophokles und Euripides* (Diss. Frankfurt, Kallmünz 1960) and W. Schmitt, *Der Deus ex machina bei Euripides* (Diss. Tübingen 1963).

86. Medeia is not a god, of course, but in this scene she certainly is intended to be more than human. For a recent treatment, see B. Knox, 'The Medea of Euripides', *YCS* 25 (1977), 193-255 = *Word and Action: Essays on the Ancient Theater* (Baltimore and London 1979), 295-322.

87. How and precisely when Dionysos made his final appearance in these two plays is uncertain. These two epiphanies will therefore not be considered in our discussion.

88.   A.P. Burnett, *Catastrophe Survived: Euripides' Plays of Mixed Reversal* (Oxford 1971), 98 n. 18, remarks that the word commanding Theoklymenos to stop (*episches*) is 'the conventional one for the interruption of a catastophe.' Nor, as she also observes, is its use confined to divine speakers — cf. Peleus at *And.* 550.

89.   Hourmouziades, 166–9, anticipated my argument in mentioning these four as 'instances where an announcement would ruin the impression of an unexpected divine intervention which the poet intends to convey by introducing an unexpected god to restrain a person from committing a violent act' (166). Arguing against Arnott, who thought that the absence of an announcement did not allow for the *mechane*, he went on to state that even among these four cases the device was certainly used in *Or.* and very probably in *Hel.*

90.   Barrett (ed.), *Hipp.*, 396 n. 1, suggests that even in these two cases where there is an announcement, the announcements 'might have been easily interpolated to suit the practice of the later theater'.

91.   Where the reaction to the earthquake 'announces' Athene.

3 PREPARATION AND SURPRISE

The element of surprise explains why several entrances that fall within an act, and therefore should be announced, are not. But the presence or absence of an announcement does not determine or indicate whether or not the entrance is surprising. Surprise is more subtle and less tangible; it is also more difficult to gauge. Surprise depends on preparation, and preparation varies in degree and kind. It is not a simple matter of a character's name, or even his impending arrival, being mentioned (although such specific reference can, of course, help to prepare for an entrance).[1] In a way, everything that precedes an entrance prepares for it.[2] The words, action, situation, mood, the whole movement of the drama leads up to and prepares in some way for that entrance. The degree of surprise that any entrance has, therefore, is unique.

In *Hel.*, after an initial recognition, Menelaos, unaware of the phantom Helen and distrusting his eyes, doubts that the woman before him is, in fact, his wife, and begins to head back to the ships. One of his servants arrives at this critical moment, explains what has happened, and brings about the true recognition of husband and wife. The messenger's entrance has not been specifically prepared for; he arrives at a crucial time; and his entrance turns about the course of events. All three factors add up to a clear example of a surprise entrance. Menelaos' entrance at *Or.* 356, on the other hand, is clearly and specifically prepared for. In the prologue, Elektra explains that he, the hope for Orestes and herself, has arrived and is expected (51ff), and her opening speech closes with her looking for his arrival (67–70). Later, in dialogue with her brother, she mentions their uncle's return and imminent arrival (241ff). His entrance, although perhaps a bit more pompous than expected, and not providing the desired help, is a surprise to no one.

The degree of surprise in some other examples is less clear cut. Theseus in *Hipp.* is away from the house, as we learn at 281. That he should return at some point is not unexpected, but the timing of his entrance — on the heels of Phaidra's suicide — is exciting and not predictable. We would not, however, call his a surprise entrance. The audience has no reason to expect Pheres' entrance at *Alk.* 614, interrupting Alkestis' funeral procession. His unwillingness to die on his son's behalf has been made clear in the first half of the play (15ff, 290ff, 338ff, 516ff), but this scene puts his son's and his own actions in a new light, causing the audience to rethink their opinion of them, Alkestis, and the whole drama. He has, nevertheless, been mentioned several times in the play and he lives nearby; should his entrance at this juncture surprise us? Again, it is a matter of degree. His arrival does not have the impact of, e.g., the servant's in *Hel.*, nor is it as clearly prepared for as Menelaos' in *Or.*

These four examples give a rough idea of the variety of preparation for and the degree of surprise in entrances. This chapter looks at some of the ways in which Euripides prepares for such entrances and the role they play in his dramas. Inevitably, the cases discussed are selective: not every entrance that is surprising in some way or to some people is included, and some that are included perhaps to some do not seem surprising. An entrance begins a scene, and how Euripides joins together his scenes — how the arrival is prepared for or not prepared for and its effect — is our concern here. Although, as stated above, every entrance and what prepares for it are unique, for discussion and comparison, entrances are considered under various categories. Chapter 4 examines and discusses the links between exits, entrances, and the songs that they frame; this chapter, therefore, focuses almost exclusively on entrances *not* directly following lyrics. Divine entrances at the end of the plays, treated briefly in Chapter 2, are considered only if there is a special twist to their introduction.

One final preliminary matter: surprising to whom? Entrances that surprise the spectators also surprise the actors, but there are several entrances for which the audience is prepared, but the actors are not. (Even in these cases, as we will see below, the audience, though informed of someone's arrival, can be surprised by some aspect of the entrance.) In what follows we are concerned primarily with the audience's response, not the actors', although the latter helps to shape the former.[3]

1. Situational Preparation/Dramatic Necessity

Several times in Euripides an entrance is preceded by no specific preparation (the character who arrives is not even mentioned), but a situation has developed that requires the arrival of this character. These entrances are surprises, and they also satisfy a dramatic need.[4]

Med. 663

The Aigeus scene in *Med.* has been criticised since antiquity.[5] The motivation he gives for his arrival (667ff) might be weak, but the audience has in a way been prepared for his appearance. No one has suggested that he might arrive; no one has even mentioned his name, but the situation in which he, or someone else to play this role, is needed has been created and dwelled on. Kreon's order of banishment has left Medeia in a quandary ('Where am I to turn?' she asks at 502 in the familiar tragic phrase). Both Medeia (387ff, 502ff, 603ff) and the chorus (359ff, 437ff, 441ff, 652ff) repeat that she is helpless and has no one to offer her shelter. Because she gave up everything for Jason, betrayed by him she has nothing left. Aigeus arrives and provides the protection that Medeia so dearly needs. The need that the drama has created and developed is met. Aigeus' entrance is a surprise, but the arrival responds to a well-defined tension in the drama and fits neatly and artfully into the play.[6]

The entrance does more than provide an answer to Medeia's plight; it suggests to Medeia her most brutal deed. Two scenes of confrontation between Medeia and Jason frame Medeia's encounter with Aigeus. After the first confrontation, Medeia threatens Jason as he exits (625-6):[7]

Be married. For perhaps — with the god's help —
You will renounce your marriage.

Although earlier in the play, the Nurse has expressed *her* concerns for the children's safety (36-7, 89-95), no threat against the children is heard here or elsewhere. Medeia's words from within at 112-14 are more a curse made in despair than an actual threat; she has used the same verb, the middle of *óllumi*, of herself at 97, and no one thinks she is contemplating suicide.[8] Her original plan for vengeance dictates the murder of Jason, his bride, and Kreon, not the children (374-5). In the second meeting with her husband, she is no longer threatening, but calmly conciliatory and deceitful. Aigeus has made the difference. Not only has he offered her a place of asylum, but he has put in her mind the murder of the children. The latter effect is achieved only indirectly, since by an awareness of the importance of Aigeus' lack of children Medeia realises the potency of murdering hers and Jason's. (The first encounter with Jason showed the importance *he* placed on the children, but she does not plan their murder until after the Aigeus scene.) Once Aigeus has departed, Medeia, in a 'tailpiece to the act, turns her attention to her vengeance with this new twist. She gives to an incredulous chorus this reason for the children's slaughter (817): 'For in this way my husband would be most stung.' And she repeats the reason to Jason in the play's finale (1370): 'These [the children] are no more. *This* will sting you'.

Hkld. 474

The implicit preparation here is not as lengthy or as marked as in *Med.*, but the same need of someone to solve a difficult situation is created and vividly depicted in Iolaos' *rhesis* (427–60). 'Where are we to turn?' he asks (440), and 'We are ruined,' he laments (442). Demophon, it seemed, had saved the day and could rescue the offspring of Herakles. But he has been thwarted by the necessity of sacrificing a girl of noble birth, a sacrifice he can ask of no Athenian. The dilemma holds small hope of solution, and the previous hope Iolaos in fact attacks (433ff). At his wits' end (*améchanos*, 472) Demophon implores Iolaos to come up with a plan. At this juncture, Makaria enters from the *skene* (she explains that she has heard them from within[9]) and offers her aid. When she learns of the crisis, she is willing to die.[10] A plan has been found, an impasse passed. The dramatic situation has found its resolution in an unprepared for, yet needed, entrance.

Ion. 1320, Hel. 597

Whereas in *Med.* the need of someone to save Medeia was heard many times and in *Hkld.* Iolaos' despair and the need of some new plan were forcefully and directly expressed before Makaria's entrance, in these two plays the implicit preparation is less marked. The frequent reminders of the need for asylum or the explicit appeal for aid are not found in these plays; rather, it is the general force of the drama that 'requires' someone's intervention to effect recognitions.

After her attempt on Ion's life, Kreousa rushes on stage and takes refuge at Apollo's altar. Soon Ion arrives and threatens to murder her in disregard of the altar's protection. Caught in the dilemma of exacting vengeance or respecting his patron's altar, he considers the injustice of the guilty being given the god's protection. The temple's priestess first found the infant Ion and reared him, Hermes explained in the prologue (41–51), and Ion refers to her in dialogue with Kreousa (318ff), but her entrance is not in any specific way prepared for, nor is the need for resolution explicitly stated. Apollo's entrance to set matters right *might* be expected by a member of the audience. Someone, the movement of the drama tells us, must intervene. Ion must not be allowed to murder his mother or to go limply off at such an impasse. The solution is provided by the priestess' entrance. 'Halt,'[11] she commands as she enters from the temple, bringing with her the tokens that allow (finally) for the recognition of mother and son.

Similarly, following the abortive recognition between Menelaos and herself in *Hel.*, Helen cannot simply be left there by her doubting husband and the couple be separated forever. Some solution must be found, we feel, but we do not know what it is. This scene is more complex than others: our expectations concerning their reunion seemed to have already been met. Euripides, however, only titillated us, raising these hopes in the first recognition only to dash them down in the doubting Menelaos. As Menelaos begins to exit (593), Helen despairs. Then the servant from the ship interrupts Menelaos' departure and informs him of the phantom Helen, who has vanished into the aether. Now Menelaos truly accepts this woman as his wife, and they enjoy a second and joyous recognition, appropriate to this strange play of doubled actions.[12]

Her. 523

In the preceding four plays, the entrance of the character was prepared for by the situation. Nothing directly prepares for the entrance, but the possibility of that entrance is not denied. In *Her.*, however, again and again we hear that Herakles' return from Hades to rescue the suppliants is impossible (e.g. 145–6, 296–97). The tension in the first third of the play lies, in part, in the conflict between the explicit denial of his arrival and the dramatic necessity of it. The almost palpable need of Herakles is created by the constant statements of his absence and inability to come back and save his family. On the level of plot, Herakles' absence in Hades has enabled Lykos to exert this power over the family. He does, of course, return in time to save his family from Lykos' butchery, an entrance that marks the first *peripeteia* of the drama. His entrance both contradicts the statements that he cannot return and satisfies the need that he return.

Or. 729

Pylades' first entrance in *Or.* perhaps is most like the servant's entrance in *Hel.* In *Hel.* and *Or.*, just when safety and recognition respectively seem guaranteed, they fall through. The servant's news in *Hel.* sets things right, but Pylades' arrival, unlike that entrance and the others, does not achieve what it promised, or at least not in the way first supposed.[13] His entrance is marvellously juxtaposed to Menelaos' exit (716). Elektra and Orestes had awaited their uncle's return; in him, they felt, lay their hope for safety (see, e.g., 68ff, 380ff, 448, 722ff). But face to face with Tyndareus, Menelaos showed his true colours and abandoned his nephew and niece. Orestes has just finished casting words at his departing uncle and begun to realise that he has been betrayed with no hope remaining (722–4) when he espies and announces his approaching companion. This entrance surprises for more than one reason. Not only does it lack specific preparation, but the act seems to have ended. After Orestes' words follow Menelaos off stage, the audience expects this long act (it began at 348) to end and the chorus to reflect on the action.[14] But Pylades overturns this expectation and introduces a new scene (accompanied by a change in metre from iambic trimeter to trochaic tetrameter). Pylades, however, for all his eagerness, offers little help. He goes along with his friends and supports his weakened comrade, but the expectation of a rescue, suggested in part by the juxtapostion to Menelaos' exit, is not fulfilled. Similar in its timing to the entrance of the 'saviour' in other plays, Pylades' entrance seems intentionally manipulated to thwart the expectations it creates. A key feature of *Or.* is the many failed attempted actions.[15] Here the unexpected arrival that in other plays offers some solution to a crisis has little effect. The 'success' of Pylades' and Orestes' scheming comes about in another and unexpected way.

2. Some Other Unexpected Entrances

The entrances already discussed were prepared for by the situation and the force of the drama. The arrival at a critical moment turned about the play's course, or, in the case of Pylades' entrance at *Or.* 729, played on the audience's expectations of its doing so. Some other unexpected entrances are not 'required' by the situation: no catastrophe is averted or recognition achieved. One could say that these unexpected entrances do not solve a puzzle but add new pieces to it.

And. 802, 881

The Nurse's[16] entrance (802) launches the second action of the drama.[17] Andromache has been rescued, and now the plot moves in a new direction: Hermione's distress and despair, her rescue by Orestes, and the murder of Neoptolemos. The new actions are punctuated by the unexpected entrances of the Nurse and Orestes. The degree of surprise in the first seems rather mild. Andromache, we do not doubt, has a Nurse (she may even be the same character as the servant seen earlier in the play — see n. 16 above); the news she has is surprising, but her entrance is only slightly so.[18] Orestes' appearance (881) is more unexpected,[19] as no mention of him has preceded his arrival *from abroad,* and the situation that developed prior to his entrance differs from what we find in other plays of rescue. The long implicit preparation that preceded, e.g. Aigeus' entrance in *Med.,* is missing. Hermione does, to be sure, feel abandoned and desires to die or to escape, but her situation does not have the same dramatic urgency as, e.g., Ion's and Kreousa's in *Ion,* especially when her lyric cries are met with the calm and sensible spoken iambics of the Nurse — she may even have begun to follow the Nurse's advice that she return to the house (876ff) when Orestes is announced. Furthermore, so soon after one rescue necessitated by her evil plots, Hermione cannot easily win the audience's sympathy and have them hope for *her* rescue. Orestes' entrance is a real surprise.

Hik. 990, 1034

Evadne makes a spectacular appearance near the end of *Hik.* (see above in Chapter 2). Her husband Kapaneus and the chorus' children are dead and the corpses have been returned, when she enters, mounts the cliff overlooking the pyre, laments her husband's death, and announces her suicide. With this entrance the focus shifts from the communal grief of the chorus to the individual sorrow of Evadne. Günther Zuntz (1955) succinctly comments: 'A short parallel within the drama, this episode echoes

in a different key that note of unending woe which resounds from
the laments of the Chorus.'[20] Iphis, her father, enters (1034), concerned about his daughter's sudden exit from the house. His
attempts to dissuade her from suicide fail and she jumps to her
death, followed by her father's expression of grief. Evadne's
entrance is not specifically prepared for, although the mention of
Kapaneus' funeral pyre (980ff) provides some link, and Iphis',
although in response to hers, is also unexpected. These two
entrances do not mark off an action as distinct as the Nurse's and
Orestes' in *And.* (and the former action is picked up again with the
entrance of the children carrying the funeral urns at 1123), but
these two entrances do move the play in an unexpected direction
in order to include another view of the war's tragedy.

In these two plays, the unexpected entrances widen the scope of
the dramas. To argue whether the plays are unified or not would
require a much fuller discussion. But we should note that
Euripides employs these surprise entrances to redirect the course
of the plays — in one, to begin a second action that in part mirrors
the first; in the other, to highlight an individual aspect of war's
pain. In both plays, the new entrances force the audience to shift
gears, as it were, and to reconsider the poet's design and their own
response to the dramas.[21]

3. Entrance of the 'Wrong' Person

Sometimes Euripides prepares the audience and the actors for an
entrance, but of someone other than the one who arrives. The
entrance is that of the 'wrong' person.

Ion 1553, IA 819, 855

Near the end of *Ion.*, the young man, shocked by Kreousa's
revelations and doubting her tale, heads towards the temple to
question Apollo. Before the entrance of the priestess at 1320, we
suggested above, one might have expected Apollo *ex machina* to
end the dilemma; now it would not be unreasonable for an experienced theatre-goer to think Apollo might enter to manage things,
as Hermes said he would in the prologue (67ff). As Ion heads for
the door, he is startled by the appearance of a divinity. Not Apollo,
though, but Athene, the 'wrong' god, appears on her brother's
behalf.

Twice, in close succession, Euripides employs the same technique in *IA*. Achilleus enters at 801, impatiently looking for Agamemnon. He begins with these questions (801–3):

Where is the leader of the Achaians?
Who of the servants would tell him
That Peleus' son Achilleus seeks him at the gates?

Such a question by an entering character is not unusual (consider, e.g., Teiresias in *Bakch.* and Menelaos in *Hel.*). But in these cases however, the persons sought enter, Kadmos and someone to open the door respectively. In *IA* Achilleus appears, seeking Agamemnon, but Klytaimestra, not the Greeks' leader, enters, explaining that she had heard his call (just as Kadmos and the old woman do).[22] This entrance is not as surprising as some others because Agamemnon, the audience knows, has left to consult with Kalchas (750). Nevertheless, there is a tension in this scene as we see Achilleus, anxious about military matters, expecting the Greeks' chieftain to appear at any moment. That Klytaimestra,[23] and not the sought Agamemnon, appears is crucial to the play's action: now Agamemnon's web of deceit begins to unravel as Achilleus reveals his ignorance of his 'engagement' to Iphigeneia. The shift in the play's movement is marked by the entrance of the 'wrong' person.

The discovery of Agamemnon's plans is still incomplete: the fraudulent marriage is clear, but the sacrifice of Iphigeneia is not. Achilleus persists in trying to find the Greeks' leader and, unaware that he is with Kalchas, declares that he will seek him inside his quarters (853–4). But an old slave stops him and bids him to wait.[24] Another surprise entrance[25] thwarts Achilleus' efforts to find Agamemnon, and more of the leader's scheme is revealed. Using the entrance of the 'wrong' person twice in such proximity, Euripides underscores the sudden turn of events, and creates a tension that builds up and reaches its peak in the inevitable encounter of husband and wife (1106ff).

Or. 71

Here both the identity and the location of the entering character are surprising. Elektra ends her prologue speech with these words (67–70):

> I look down every road, hoping to see
> Menelaos approaching. Since otherwise on weak
> Strength are we anchored, unless we are saved
> By him. A house in bad times is helpless.

She probably accompanies these lines with glances down the two *parodoi*, expectant of Menelaos' imminent return. Perhaps the audience follows suit, looking for and expecting Menelaos to arrive and save this helpless pair. But Menelaos does not at that moment enter down the *parodos*, nor does anyone else. From the *skene*, not the *parodos*, Helen, not her husband, appears. Elektra meets not with their potential rescuer, but the ultimate cause of all their suffering. In a play of many surprises, this entrance helps to establish the mood. It might also suggest that the hope that the children have in Menelaos will prove futile: just as here Elektra looks literally and figuratively to Menelaos and finds not him but Helen, so later when he does arrive, his presence is useless to his kin.

4. Surprises of Location

Helen's entrance at *Or.* 71 is surprising in both the character and the location. The place of entry at *Ion* 1553 also surprises the audience, since Ion heads for the temple doors (and the audience's eyes follow) and then Athene appears on high. On at least two other occasions Euripides surprised the audience with the place (and perhaps the timing) of the entrance; both involve someone moving towards and trying to enter the *skene* door, interrupted by the appearance of another from above.

Med. 1317, Or. 1567[26]

Jason, seeking to avenge Medeia's murder of Glauke and Kreon, rushes on stage, where he learns of the children's murder inside. He orders that the doors be opened and threatens to punish Medeia. Our attention has been drawn to the doors when Medeia appears on high in her chariot,[27] triumphant and in command (1317–18):

> Why are you disturbing and monkeying with these doors,
> Seeking the corpses and me, the murderer?

Page (ed.), *ad loc.*, observes that *anamochleúō* (which I translate 'monkey with' to suggest its unusualness) is a very rare word. It is first attested here and not found again until Lucian. The bold language, then, underlines the bold stage action of Medeia's sudden and remarkable appearance in her chariot.[28]

Or. presents a very similar situation. Menelaos arrives in response to what he has heard of Orestes' murderous activities. Like Jason, he demands that the doors be opened and threatens to kill his nephew and accomplice. As in *Med.*, our attention focuses on the door. What effect will Menelaos' efforts and threats have, we wonder? But before the doors can be opened, Orestes appears on the roof and gives *his* command (1567–8):

> *You*, don't touch these doors with your hand.
> I command you, Menelaos, who have built yourself up with daring.

Is there a pun in these words which, like the choice of *anamochleúo* in *Med.*, reinforces the striking entrance? *Pepúrgōsai* which is translated 'have built yourself up', comes from *purgóō* which literally means 'to fortify with towers'. Although almost always metaphorical in tragedy (but see, e.g., *Bakch.* 172), so close to *kléithrōn* ('doors'), perhaps it should be taken paronomastically.

This scene has, of course, a visually spectacular finale, where the playwright goes one step beyond the impressive ending of *Med.* To the double-tiered action of Menelaos on the ground and Orestes and others on the roof is added a third level with Apollo's appearance (1625). Unlike Medeia, although Orestes may seem to have taken over the divine role, he has not, and his final action also turns out differently than planned. We might also observe a 'visual turnabout' in this scene. In the only other encounter between Orestes and Menelaos, Orestes lay on the ground as Menelaos entered in a pompous and indifferent manner. Here Orestes is elevated (literally and in terms of apparent power) and Menelaos is on the ground.

5. 'Talk of the Devil'

Athene's entrance at *Tro.* 48 is, we have seen, linked to the preceding scene by Poseidon's mention in his departing lines of her destruction of Troy. Although her appearance is a great surprise, Euripides subtly joins together the two scenes with this verbal link. Other entrances, not all of them surprising, are similarly linked to the preceding scenes; we will call them 'talk of the devil' entrances.[29] Under this heading are included entrances that are preceded by the mention or hint of the new arrival's name, whether the arrival is expected or not, when this mentioning creates a special tension or highlights a surprise. Excluded are the many cases of someone asking, e.g., 'Where is the king?', and then that questioner or another announcing the arrival (e.g. *Hipp.* 1153ff, *IT* 1153ff). This is but a convenient way of introducing a new character and is of neutral value. Also excluded are such entrances that follow a lyric; they are treated in the next chapter.

IA 1106ff

Only once in Euripides does a character actually say something like 'talk of the devil'. In *IA* Klytaimestra, now aware of her husband's murderous schemes, comes forth from the *skene* looking for him, and, when she spots him says (1103–5):

> I was just mentioning him who approaches,
> Agamemnon here, who at once will be found out
> Plotting impious deeds against his own children.

The confrontation between the two has been inevitable since Agamemnon's plans unravelled in the previous scene (see above), and the audience awaits the conflict that his return brings. Unlike the examples mentioned above, this technique is not of neutral dramatic value: bringing the confrontation into sharper focus increases the tension in this scene.

Bakch. 1211ff

When Agave returns triumphant, displaying the head of her prey to the city, she asks for her father and, with painful irony, her son, in order to show off her prize (1211–12):

> Where is the old man, my father? Let him come near.
> And Pentheus, my son, where is he?

She then commands someone to fasten her booty to the triglyphs.

As if in response to her questions, Kadmos enters at 1216 with attendants carrying Pentheus' remains. The scene of false triumph is thus neatly linked to the scene of joyless revelation. The effect of the scene is prolonged as no contact is made between the two until 1231, when Kadmos sees his daughter.[30] In performance, Agave might look here and there on stage while Kadmos enters and relates his sad tale from the mountains.

Hel. 546

Menelaos goes into hiding at 514, before the chorus and Helen return from the *skene*. After a brief choral song (515–27), Helen begins her return to Proteus' tomb and reflects on Theonoe's predictions. Her husband is alive, even somewhere in the land, but where and in what condition, she does not know. Finally she turns to address the thought-to-be-absent Menelaos (540): 'Oh my! When will you come? Your return is greatly desired.' No sooner does she finish with her appeal to her husband than she notices someone and thinks she is being attacked. Of course, it proves to be Menelaos; her question and her wish are fulfilled. This 'entrance' does not surprise the audience — they have seen him go into hiding, and perhaps they smile as Helen wonders about him and wishes he would come. The clever link and the timing of the 'entrance' add to the light touch in this scene.[31]

Ion 1250

After the attempt to poison Ion fails and the plot is uncovered, the chorus in a brief astrophic song (1229–43) bemoans the punishment that awaits them and Kreousa. Then in anapests (1244–9) they turn to ask what more can Kreousa suffer (1246–47):

> What, poor mistress, remains
> For your spirit to suffer?

As observed in Chapter 2, these words do not address Kreousa, who rushes on stage immediately after the anapests. Rather they serve as a 'talk of the devil' link. What more remains for Kreousa to suffer? With her arrival the question begins to be answered.

El. 761ff

One 'talk of the devil' entrance clearly shows Euripides self-consciously playing with dramatic conventions. After her brother has left to murder Aigisthos in *El.*, Elektra frets and worries that the venture will fail. She hears a shout and fears the worse, ignoring the advice of the cautious chorus (758–60):

> *Ch.* Hold on, so you may know your fortunes clearly.
> *El.* It's not possible. We are beaten. For where are the messengers?
> *Ch.* They will come. It's no small thing to kill a king.

If they were victorious, the messengers would have already arrived with the news, as they always do after such events, she reasons (and Euripides slyly reminds us). The messenger with the news immediately follows (761). The expectations of a messenger's entrance are met, but only after the playwright draws attention to those expectations.[32]

And. 1070

The messenger's entrance at *And.* 1070 is a sort of 'talk of the devil' in reverse. When Peleus learns of the plot to kill his grand-son, he wants to send a messenger to Delphi (1066–9):

> Oh my! This is dreadful. Won't someone
> As quickly as possible go to the Pythian altar
> And tell friends there what is planned,
> Before the child of Achilleus is killed by his enemies?

One of Peleus' attendants may begin to exit; maybe he does not even have time for that. It is too late in any case. Instead of a messenger leaving for Delphi, one arrives from there exclaiming (1070–1):

> Oh my!
> Unhappy I am to announce such turns of fortune
> To you, old man, and to my master's friends.

No one will explain the events to friends there (*toîs ekeî léxei philois* 1068), but someone will report to friends here (*angelôn ... philoisi, 1070–1*). A further verbal echo links the scenes: both Peleus and the messenger begin with a cry of woe (*oimoi,* 1066 and *ṓmoi moi,* 1070).[33]

Notes

1. Taplin's discussions on preparation, *passim* and esp. the introductory remarks, 9–12, are very useful (see also the bibliographic footnote, 65 n. 3). He too points to the limitations of restricting preparation to the mentioning of a character, limitations well illustrated in T.B.L. Webster, 'Preparation and Motivation in Greek Tragedy', *CR* 47 (1933), 117–23.

2. We should also observe that what a character says and does *after* he arrives, including the motivation he might give for his entrance, also affects the way we view the entrance. In what follows we are concerned primarily with what precedes the entrance, the preparation for the action that begins with the new entrance.

3. One could say much more about the actors' responses, the ways in which they differ from the audience's and the connections between the two. Unfortunately, this extends beyond the scope of our study.

4. On 'dramatic necessities' and story patterns in Greek tragedy, see R. Lattimore, *Story Patterns in Greek Tragedy* (Ann Arbor 1964). His approach is picked up to some degree by A.P. Burnett, *Catastrophe Survived: Euripides' Plays of Mixed Reversal* (Oxford 1971). Taplin, *passim*, also discusses situational preparation, and (11 n. 1) points to Aigeus' entrance in *Med.* as an example in Euripides.

5. See Aristole, *Poetics* 1461b, 19–21 and the scholion at *Med.* 666. On the Aigeus scene, see T.V. Buttrey, 'Accident and Design in Euripides' '*Medee.*', *AJP* 79 (1958) 1–17.

6. Page (ed.), xxxix, reminds us that we do not know whether this encounter between the two was traditional or not. If not, it is noteworthy that Euripides underscores the innovation with a dramatic surprise.

7. On the convention of words cast at a departing character's back which he does not hear, see Taplin, 'Significant Actions in Sophocles' *Philocletes*', *GRBS* 12 (1971), 42 and n. 39, *Stagecraft*, 221–2, D. Bain, *Actors and Audiences: A Study of Asides and Related Conventions in Greek Tragedy* (Oxford 1977), 34 and n. 4, and Mastronarde, 30, 110.

8. Cf. *óloito* at *Hipp*, 407 Barrett's (ed.), *ad loc.*, calls it, 'so stereotyped a formula'.

9. Taplin, 220, includes this entrance among those in response to cries of grief or distress. It resembles those to an extent, but, unlike the others, this entrance is a great surprise.

10. On the motif of self-sacrifice in Euripides, see the bibliography cited by Collard (ed.), *Supplices*, vol. 2, 354–5, and recently on human sacrifice in Greek religion, A. Henrichs, 'Human Sacrifice in Greek Religion: Three Case Studies' in *Le sacrifice dans l'antiquité*, Entretiens sur l'antiquité classique, 27 (Vandoeuvres-Geneva 1981), 195–22.

11. The word used is *episches*; see Chapter 2 n. 88.

12. On this scene see W. Ludwig, *Sapheneia: Ein Beitrag zur Formkunst im Spätwerk des Euripides* (Diss. Stuttgart 1954), 105–9.

13. The 'failure' of Pylades differs from the actions of Herakles in *Her.* Herakles does accomplish what the situation required and his entrance promised — he rescues the family. Only later is there a violent *peripeteia* that turns rescue to catastrophe.

14. Burnett (above n. 4), 186, also observes this.

15. On this feature of the play and on this scene, see Burnett's articulate discussion, 183–204.

16. See Stevens (ed.), *ad loc.*, for the problems of this character's identification — Nurse or servant.

17. For a summary of the many attempts to solve the problem of unity in this play, see H. Erbse, 'Euripides' "Andromache"', *Hermes* 94 (1966), 276–97. See W. Friedrich, *Euripides und Diphilos*, Zetemata 5 (Munich 1953), 47 ff, for Euripides' blending of the two actions (one old, one new) in both *And.* and *Hek.*

18. Taplin, 11–12, observes that an entrance can be surprising if only *some* aspect of it has not been prepared for. While this is correct in principle, we should be careful not to consider surprising all entrances some aspects of which have not been prepared for; otherwise, the entrances of all messengers with their news and of many other characters would be thought surprising. Perhaps the best example in Euripides of an entrance not prepared for in all its aspects is the Phrygian's at *Or.* 1369. After Helen's shouts from within and the tricking of Hermione into the *skene*, a variation on a familiar pattern (see Chapter 4), the audience expects someone to enter with the report of what has happened within. But no one could have expected the unusual entrance of the Phrygian slave, his exciting aria, and the peculiar news that Helen has disappeared.

19. On Orestes' entrance Mastronarde, 26, makes an interesting observation: 'When Orestes later reveals that he had been aware of the situation at the palace and had been waiting "in the wings," some members of the audience might perhaps assume that Orestes himself had been conspicuously manipulating arrival-conventions in order to induce Hermione to welcome him as her savior.'

20. G. Zuntz, *The Political Plays of Euripides* (Manchester 1955), 12. See his sensitive discussion of the play, 3–25.

21. Other entrances might fairly be considered here: e.g. Pheres' at *Alk.* 614, touched on briefly in the opening of this chapter. An entrance very similar in some ways to those discussed in this section is Menelaos' in *Tro.*, which introduces a new element into the drama, marked by the 'second prologue' delivered by Menelaos; but this entrance and the Helen scene it begins are not particularly surprising. See the discussion of *Tro.* in Chapter 5.

22. This further suggests that Euripides plays on the expectations of the more usual entrance after someone knocks on the door or calls to those within.

23. Is it fanciful to see an echo here of her entrance at Aisch. *Cho.* 668? In *Cho.* another young man, a disguised Orestes, comes to the door, emphasising that he wants to talk to the *man* in charge; Klytaimestra then appears at the *skene* door. The switching of sex roles is a theme of the trilogy, first suggested in the prologue of *Ag.*, 10–11.

24. The staging of this scene raises problems: how many doors does the *skene* have? what does *púlas paroíxas* (857) mean? See Hourmouziades, 21–2. However the scene is staged, the effect will be fundamentally the same.

25. Hamilton, as indicated in Chapter 2 n. 65, considers this an 'Ersatz' announcement. But its only proper parallel, someone coming from the *skene* in response to noise on stage, is Makaria's entrance at *Hkld.* 474, which is clearly surprising.

26. These two entrances, in addition to other 'unexpected' features in Euripides, are discussed in G. Arnott, 'Euripides and the Unexpected', G & R Second Series 20 (1973), 49–64.

27. N.E. Collinge, 'Medea *Ex Machina*', *CP* 57 (1962), 171, remarks, 'we are all — audience, chorus, Jason and attendants — wildly misled at the moment of Medea's final entrance.'

28. Page (ed.), *ad loc.*, comments on the mark this line left on posterity, as judged by parodies and imitations, and he suggests that the combination of the word with the context of its delivery, 'would make the innovation more noticeable and memorable'.

29. On 'talk of the devil' entrances and distinctions within them, see Taplin, 137–8, who uses the phrase somewhat differently from the way I do. With his

more restricted definition, he grants for Euripides only three 'examples of a sort': *El.* 761, *Bakch* 1216, *IA* 1106. Add *Med.* 1121 to those I discuss in this section.
30. See Mastronarde, 25, on this entrance and the gradual contact.
31. On this 'entrance' and other 'clever' elements in Euripides, see R.P. Winnington-Ingram, 'Euripides: Poiētēs Sophos', *Arethusa* 2 (1969), 129–42.
32. Winnington-Ingram, 131–2, also discusses the self-consciousness of this passage.
33. Uncertainties mar discussion of two passages. The servant who addresses Hippolytos (*Hipp.* 88ff) comes from where — from the band that attends Hippolytos (Wilamowitz, ed.)? from the 'background' (Taplin, 90)? from the *skene*? Hourmouziades (18–19) makes a suggestion deserving serious consideration: the servant, hearing the returning hunters, opens the door for them, and, hence, comes into contact with Hippolytos. However the entrance is staged, it is not especially surprising and it does not greatly alter the course of events, although the servant's advice serves as a useful foil to Hippolytos' views on Aphrodite. The identity of the one who opposes Theoklymenos in *Hel.* remains unknown. Messenger (Campbell, ed.), coryphaeus (Kannicht and Dale, eds.), and servant (most recently, D.P. Stanley-Porter, 'Who Opposes Theoclymenus?', *CP* 72 (1977), 45–8) have all been put forth as candidates. Whoever it is, this sudden opposition is quite extraordinary. *If* this opposition involves an entrance, it certainly is a surprising one, and, although it does not stop Theoklymenos, it does offer, with the following appearance of the Dioskouroi, a contrast between human and divine power.

4 ENTRANCES, EXITS AND SONGS

Euripides did not compose *embólima* for his tragedies; Agathon did. So Aristotle informs us in a celebrated passage of the *Poetics*[1]. In the same passage he recommends that the chorus help the poet in the competition, i.e., that it sing integrally related songs, as in Sophokles, not as in Euripides.[2] To what extent Euripides' choral songs are not integrally related to the rest of the dramas has been much debated.[3] The standard history of Greek literature offers a balanced view: Euripides' odes, with the exception of the 'Demeter ode' in *Hel.*, are all more or less closely connected with the action of the drama.[4] In other words, the songs and acts of Euripides' plays are connected, but the reader who always expects from Euripides the tight and neat construction of, e.g., Sophokles' *OT*, will be disappointed.

A lyric[5] can be related to the 'action' in numerous ways. Our concern in this chapter, however, is not the general connections between songs and episodes, nor is it the broad thematic unity of the dramas.[6] I plan to investigate a narrower field: how odes are connected specifically to the following entrance and, to a lesser degree, the preceding exit. Taplin's theory, described earlier, states that the basic structural pattern involves the rearrangement of actors by means of exits and entrances around songs. Connections between songs and entrances and exits should, therefore, be expected, and a study of them informative.

I do not imply that such dramatic links can or should be severed entirely from thematic ones: the two are interwoven. When, e.g., in *Her.* Iris and Lyssa appear (822) immediately after the joyous song proclaiming the gods' justice, it is not only a theatrical *tour de force*, but thematically important as well. The way Euripides structured his plays reveals a great deal about their meaning, and the links he made at the important junctures of song and entrance and exit inform us about the larger issues of the dramas. Our focus will be on these links.

Characters do not merely enter or exit; they take part in the action, immediately or belatedly, when they arrive on stage; we cannot separate completely the entrance of a character from his subsequent actions. Thus, some of our observations would be little changed if we did not focus on entrances and exits as the point of contact with the odes. By limiting our scope, however, we can take advantage of looking at the very joints, as it were, of the plays, and make more specific observations as a result.

How, then, does an ode lead up to and prepare for the following entrance and how does it respond to the preceding exit? What are the connections? Frequently there is no special one between the song and the stage action, and not all songs are treated. For example, when Theseus returns at *Hik.* 381 after the chorus praises Argos and prays to Pallas, there is no particular link between the song and the entrance. Nor does Theoklymenos' entrance at *Hel.* 1165 have a special connection to the preceding ode, which concludes with a vivid description of the destruction caused by Helen.[7] But often the song leads us to expect the entrance, to be surprised by it, to interpret it in a certain light — or to reinterpret the song. Verbal echoes also serve to connect the lyric and spoken parts of the plays. Specific connections between lyrics and preceding exits are less frequent, and they will receive less attention.[8]

A play by play analysis, although it provides a definite framework for discussing these connections, would be less effective. To examine these links by groups or types allows the observation of similar technique in different plays, but the divisions are to a degree artificial. I assume the risks of the latter method. The groupings are, ultimately, arbitrary. They do not represent precise differences in the poet's thinking, and some connections fall into more than one category; but they do seem to indicate some basic ways in which entrances and exits are linked to the songs. They are illustrative and suggestive, not restrictive. The three broad groupings that I use are: (1) surprise and contrast; (2) verbal links; (3) prayers and predictions.

1. Surprise and Contrast

Odes of False Preparation

Euripides wrote several songs in which the chorus proclaims one thing and the following entrance displays another, even the very opposite. Such odes of false preparation (*parà prosdokian*), ones which prepare the audience for the opposite of what, in fact, proves to be the case, have been denied for Euripides,[9] but I think that the following examples verify their existence.

At *Alk.* 861 Admetos and the chorus re-enter in the 'epiparo-dos'. In the following one-actor scene Admetos finally realises the implications of Alkestis' sacrifice, and he cannot bear to enter the house. In an attempt at consolation, the chorus sings that nothing is stronger than Necessity (965). Even the sons of the gods are subject to death (989–90). (Perhaps at this point, despite Apollo's prediction (65–9) and Herakles' own claims (837–60), we doubt his ability to win Alkestis' release?) The chorus then shifts from the general statement of Necessity's power to the specific case of Admetos, whom it addresses in the second strophic pair.[10] The chorus concludes that Alkestis will be addressed by wayfarers as a *daimōn* (1000–05):

> And someone, stepping off onto a side path,
> Will say this:
> 'She died at one time on her husband's behalf.
> And now she is a blessed spirit.
> Greetings, lady, and look kindly on us.'
> Such words will address her.

Hardly are these words spoken when Herakles enters leading in Alkestis, who, recently returned from the dead, veiled and mute, is, in fact, something of a *daimōn.* An ode that in part was intended to enable Admetos to exit into his house is followed by Herakles' entrance. Herakles' triumphant return with Alkestis (the audience, at any rate, knows at once who is with him) proves that what was said to be impossible *is* possible. The striking juxtaposition of song and entrance underlines life's capacity to overcome death (at least temporarily).[11] A.M. Dale (1954) puts it well in her commentary (p. 119):

> The tragic thread is now complete; enter Herakles with the veiled Alcestis, and in a triumphant peripety the happy-fairy-tale thread comes uppermost. Not that Anangke or our hard-won wisdom is fallible; it is our understanding of the design of Necessity at any given time that may be faulty; the god has found a way where it seemed no way was: *tôn d'adokētōn póron heûre theós.*

In *Her.* there are two startling turnabouts. In the first (discussed in Chapter 3) Herakles rescues his family from death at Lykos' hands; in the second, the triumphant saviour is changed into the crazed murderer of his kin. The second switch is made doubly unexpected and dramatically effective by two preceding odes that praise his return and vengeance on Lykos. The first ode, sung before Lykos is murdered, hymns Youth and, directly and indirectly, Herakles.[12] After the tyrant enters the house and meets his fatal punishment, the chorus breaks forth in joyous song, extolling the victory of Herakles and justice. The ode concludes (809–14):

> You were a better ruler to me
> Than that ignoble Lykos,
> As is now clear to anyone
> Who looks on the contest of swords,
> If justice still is pleasing to the gods.

Amid the joy there is at least the possibility of doubt;[13] the conditional clause at the end of the stasimon seems rhetorical, but it raises the question of the lack of divine justice (a charge made frequently in the play, e.g. at 339ff and 498ff). The dominant mood, however, is one of celebration and joy. The mood is shattered at once (815–16):

> Ah! Ah!
> Do we all now have the same fear,
> Old men, since I see such a phantom above the house?

The chorus is startled; joy has turned to fear. What was assumed to be rhetorical becomes an open question. Iris and Lyssa, it proves to be, have arrived to madden Herakles into killing his children. The joy of the ode has been shown wrong: the gods are not just; they have again taken control of Herakles' life.

A sequence of song and entrance in *Hkld.* is not as surprising as the two just observed, but the pattern is fundamentally the same. The first stasimon (353–80) serves basically as a lyric restatement of what has transpired in the previous scene,[14] and it re-enforces the optimistic mood. The chorus proclaims its confidence in Athens after Demophon puts the Argive herald to rout and promises his city's aid. The mood is extinguished immediately by Demophon's return directly after the ode. Before he even says a word, we know that something is amiss, because, contrary to convention,[15] Iolaos, not Demophon, the oncoming character, speaks first 381–2):

> Child, why do you come with your face full of anxiety?
> Will you say something new about the battle?

Demophon explains that he cannot supply the aid he had promised; he will not kill an Athenian child as the oracle commands. The hopes built up in the previous scene, and reasserted in the ode, are dashed upon Demophon's arrival. But they will be raised again by Makaria's heroic and surprising entrance at 474.

In two plays the entrance that overturns the statement and mood of the ode does not follow it immediately. In both *And.* and *Her.* a saviour arrives in the middle of an act, but it seems best to discuss them here because the entrances clearly show the songs 'false' and the action following the odes and leading up to the entrance is, in a sense, an extension of the previous action, building the tension until the rescuers arrive.

Before the second stasimon of *And.* (464–93), Andromache yields to Menelaos' threats, issued on Hermione's behalf, and everyone but the chorus exits into the *skene*. Death awaits Andromache, and maybe her son. In a typical lyric progression, the movement of thought in the song is from the general to the specific case of the present. The general observation that to have two rivals for one person is disastrous, supported by parallels in other spheres, is then demonstrated by the current example of Hermione, who, the chorus proclaims, is going to kill Andromache and child (486ff). After the song the chorus announces the 'moving tableau' of Andromache and her son, condemned to death (494ff). The victims lament their fate (singing in glyconics and pherecrateans) and plead with Menelaos, who responds in anapests. His final and seemingly definitive statement of their doom (537–44) is met by Peleus' timely arrival as the protector of his kin. His entrance, although timely, is not as surprising as some others, since the expectations of his appearance began when Andromache sent the Nurse to bring him (83ff). Neither the chorus nor the audience, however, knows that he will appear in time to save the threatened pair, and his arrival thwarts the deaths predicted in the ode and lamented in the following lyrics.

A very similar pattern of action is found in *Her.* (Herakles' entrance at 523 is treated with a different emphasis in the previous chapter.) As in *And.*, the intended victims and their persecutor exit before the ode. Here Lykos exits down the *parodos*, while Herakles' family enters the *skene* to don proper garments for their slaughter. The chorus is inspired to sing the labours of Herakles. The final labour involves the descent into Hades, from which, the chorus emphasises, he has not returned (425ff). The ode finishes with the focus on the children and the old men's inability to defend them (436–41):

> If I had the strength of my youth
> And could wield the spear in battle,
> With my young Theban comrades,
> I would champion the children.
> But as things are now, I lack my blessed youth.

The scene opens with the entrance of these children, their mother and grandfather. The mention of the children near the end of the song (430ff), in the ode's familiar shift towards the present, prepares us for their entrance. This reference, coupled with the chorus' regret of lack of youthful vigour, depicts their plight as they enter: one group is too young, the other is too old; Herakles is needed. Herakles does, of course, appear, but not until another sixty lines of trimeters are spoken. Whereas in *And.* we witness laments and pleas, contrasted with Menelaos' orders, here we listen to narrative and reflective speeches expressing their despair. (There is the luxury of full *rhesis* in *Her.* because the persecutor is not on stage.) Herakles then enters and the rescue is achieved. His arrival contradicts the first stasimon (and the first part of the play); Herakles did go down into Hades, but it is not his 'final' labour, only his most recent. To summarise the similarities between these two sequences of action in *And.* and *Her.*: suppliants exit into the *skene*; an ode follows which ends with a mention of or allusion to the imminent murders; the suppliants re-enter; the slaughter is delayed; the protector finally arrives, overturning the ode's statements of gloom.[16]

The *Hipp.* shows a milder 'ode of false preparation'. Banished by his father, Hippolytos bids farewell to Athens and departs with his followers. The chorus then expresses its confusion over the injustice of Hippolytos' punishment and its grief over his exile, concluding (1148–50):

Yoked Graces, why do you send away
From his fatherland, away from this house,
This wretched man, who has no blame in this ruin?

They make no mention of Theseus' curse (895–6), in which he prayed that Poseidon kill Hippolytos; they respond only to the alternative punishment — Theseus' pronouncement of exile (897–8), the sole possibility that Theseus mentions in Hippolytos' presence. In this part of the play the poet suppresses any reference to the other possibility — Hippolytos' death, which is predicted by Aphrodite in the prologue — so that the messenger's report of Hippolytos' fantastic end is all the more dramatically effective.

Implicit Preparation

Herakles' first appearance in *Alk.* and Aigeus' in *Med.* respond to their preceding odes in a different way. We discussed in Chapter 3 the concept of implicit preparation — characters for whom a strong need is created, but no specific preparation is made. In *Alk.* of course, Apollo predicts Herakles' arrival in his prologue speech; so the audience, but not the characters, expects him to come at some point. Euripides underscores that expectation by implicitly preparing for his entrance in the ode immediately preceding it.

The first stasimon of *Alk.* (435–75) both responds to the preceding exit and prepares for the following entrance. Alkestis perishes on stage and Admetos exits with her corpse. The chorus then sings the praises of Alkestis, claiming that her fame will spread above and below the earth. As we saw in *Hkld.* 353ff, the ode to a great extent repeats sentiments already expressed in the play.[17] With her death the first movement of the drama is over, and the ode lyrically emphasises what has transpired. But the ode moves forward also. At the beginning of the second strophe, the song takes a new tack to praising Alkestis — the chorus wishes they could bring her back (455–9):

I wish I could,
I wish I had the power to send you
From the realms of Hades
And the streams of Kokytos,
Plying an oar on the underworld's river.

They cannot bring Alkestis back from the dead. But Herakles, who

Apollo has predicted would do just that, can, and he arrives directly after the ode. One might object that the chorus' wish serves only as further praise of their mistress and occurs too far removed from Herakles' entrance (476). The wish, however, is vivid in its repeated form, and the prologue has made the audience, at any rate, alert to the implicit contrast between the chorus' and Herakles' powers. With Herakles' entrance the contrast becomes clear. Later in the play when Herakles returns with Alkestis and Admetos explains his actions in a *rhesis*, Herakles' first statement to Admetos, albeit a deceitful one, echoes the chorus' earlier words of helplessness (1072–4):

> Would that I had the power to bring back your wife
> To the light from the house of the underworld
> And to do you this favour.

Note the similarities in the wish for the power (*dúnamin*, 1072/ *dunaímạn*, 456) to bring back Alkestis to the light (*es phôs*, 1073/ *pháos* (accusative of motion), 457) from the underworld (*nertérōn*, 1073/ *nertérai*, 459).

We described in Chapter 3 Aigeus' entrance at *Med.* 663. Our focus here is not on how it responds to the general needs of the drama, but how, more specifically, the song prepares for it. After her first confrontation with Jason, Medeia casts these words at him as he exits (623–6):[18]

> Go. You are gone from the house for a while
> And you are seized with desire for your new young wife.
> Be married. For perhaps — with the god's help—
> You will renounce your marriage.

Medeia claims that it is desire (*póthōi*, 623) for his new bride that draws Jason away, and her final words contain a threat against his new marriage (*gameîs* 'you are married' and *gámon* 'marriage' emphatically frame the final line). It is with this destructive force of love that the chorus begins the second stasimon, praying that it might not come to them (627–30):

> Passions coming in excess
> Give man not a good name nor virtue.

After Medeia's reaction to Jason's betrayal and this reference to Jason's *póthos* the chorus' song is ambiguous: 'passions' seem to refer to both Medeia and Jason. As in *Alk.* 435ff, the ode looks forward as well as back; antistrophe b focuses on Medeia's plight (655–62):

> You no city, no friend
> Pitied, when you suffered
> The most terrible of sufferings.
> May he die miserably, whoever
> Does not hold his friends in honour,
> Revealing his honest mind;
> To me he will never be a friend.

The implicit preparation for Aigeus, made many times prior to the ode, is forcefully made here at the end of the song. (This ending also contains a not-very-veiled attack on Jason.) Aigeus arrives at 663 in marked contrast to Jason, and he provides the aid that Medeia sorely needs.[19] Medeia's lack of a *philos* is made emphatic by the threefold repetition of the word in the ode's closing lines (655, 660, 662). Aigeus is the *philos* Medeia needs, and he makes it clear in his first words that he is her *philos* (663–4):

> Medeia, greetings. I say this for no one knows
> A fairer way than this to address *friends*.

The word *philos* also helps to make clear the difference between Jason and Aigeus. The former had claimed that he was Medeia's *philos* when he first arrived (459ff) and in his parting words (621–2). But Aigeus, not Jason, shows by deed that he is her *philos*. We observed in Chapter 3 that Aigeus' entrance responds to a dramatic need and alters the course of events. This entrance also is neatly linked to the ode, and thus the entrance and its subsequent effects — this is the turning point of the drama — are underscored by the juxtaposition.

Image and Action

An image or scene described in an ode can have a vivid counterpart on stage. What the audience first experiences in words (and gestures) is recreated, in a sense, in a striking stage action that begins with the following entrance.[20] Or, as is the case in *El.*, the stage action is vividly echoed in the opening of the next lyric. In all but one of the following cases the juxtaposition of image and action produces a contrast. The example from *Tro.* depicts the continuation of the war's horrors rather than any contrast, but it is treated with the other cases.

Two plays about the Trojan War employ this type of juxtaposition to heighten the pathos of the war. In *Hek.* a brief stasimon is sung after Polyxene's death and Hekabe's lamentation over it (629–57). The stasimon seeks the beginning of ills in the Judgement of Paris: from this came suffering upon suffering. The emphasis falls on Trojan griefs, but the final lines paint a picture of a Spartan mother lamenting her dead offspring (652–7):

> And a Spartan girl also grieves with many tears in her home,
> Near the fair-flowing Eurotas,
> And a mother over her dead children strikes her greying head
> And bloodies her cheek with her nails.

Immediately after these lines are sung the servant who had been sent to bring water for Polyxene's corpse returns with Polydoros' newly discovered body.[21] (See Chapter 2 for another view of this entrance.) The grief we witness now is of no Spartan woman, but of Hekabe over her own son. The song's closing suggestion that war causes suffering for both sides is undercut by this entrance. War does bring suffering to both sides, but this play focuses on Hekabe's griefs and how they quite literally dehumanise her. The graphic juxtaposition of image and action forcefully underscores *Hekabe's* woes. The 'second action' of the drama begins with this entrance. Euripides is the first poet we know of to bring together the stories of Polyxene and Polydoros;[22] he links the two stories in many ways[23] and initiates the second movement of the drama (predicted in the prologue) with a vivid contrast between the ode's closing image and the entrance of Polydoros' corpse, a contrast that connects the two actions in Hekabe's suffering over them.

The first stasimon of *Tro.* (511–67) is inspired by Hekabe's pronouncement before the ode (509–10):

> Of the prosperous
> Consider no one fortunate, until he dies.

The choristers sing of *their* change of fortune the night Troy fell.

Having painted a picture of the joy and celebration that accompanied the reception of the horse into the city, they turn in the epode to the bloodshed that followed, enumerating individual horrors, the first one of which is the suffering of children (557–9):

> And dear infants
> Were throwing their frightened arms
> Around their mothers' robes.

After the song, the chorus announces Andromache and Astyanax being led away in a wagon (568–71):

> Hekabe, do you see Andromache here,
> Carried in on the enemy's cart?
> And her own Astyanax, Hektor's son,
> Is at her heaving breast.

A variation of the scene depicted in the ode is enacted in the following entrance: the suffering brought about by Troy's fall goes on, as children still cling to their mothers. The implicit contrast between the more common royal chariot entrance and the fallen princess and son in a humble wagon adds to the impact of the entrance.[24] The suffering suggested by the juxtaposition will, of course, reach yet another level in this act when Talthybios enters and demands the murder of the young boy.

In other instances the image in the song refers to a definite event in the past. The juxtaposition of the visual picture of the entrance and that of the lyric is thus additionally charged by the mytho-historical comparison.

We have already discussed Medeia's surprising entrance at *Med.* 1317. Although her entrance does not follow the ode immediately, she is the focus of Jason's and the audience's attention once the former enters seeking to punish her, and her appearance with her two slain children is decidedly coloured by the ode's final stanza. In this stanza (directly following the cries of the children from within) the chorus compares Medeia to Ino, who, maddened by the gods, killed her children and died along with them (1289). Ino, self-sacrificing and driven to her murder by the gods (1284), contrasts starkly with the living, triumphant Medeia. The scholiast *ad loc.* relates that in the more usual version of the tale, one of Ino's sons is murdered by his father.[25] Euripides, then, seems to have chosen a less common version of the myth to sharpen the contrast between Medeia and the mythological *exemplum*.

In *And.* Hermione exits at 268, threatening Andromache's life, and the latter concludes the scene with general comments on the wickedness of women. The following choral song reverts to the Judgement of Paris and then to his birth as the ultimate source of the present problems. 'This song has no direct relevance to the dramatic situation, but, as often in plays dealing with some aspect of the Trojan legend, the chorus or actors go back to the *archḕ kakȭn* ...' Such is the verdict of P.T. Stevens (ed.), *ad loc.* It is certainly characteristic of a Euripidean chorus to find the cause of current troubles in past events,[26] but this ode has specific and carefully constructed links to the drama; it does more than provide background for the present crisis. The second strophe, after the first strophic pair bemoaned the Judgement, is devoted to the wish that Hekabe, following Kassandra's mantic advice, had killed the infant Paris. In the final stanza (antisrophe b) the chorus, making the familiar shift from past to present with an address to Andromache (302), concludes with contrary-to-fact statements that would be true *if* Paris had been killed. They close with these words (307–8):

And beds would not have been left empty and abandoned,
And aged parents be bereft of their children.

The special relevance of both the lengthy wish that the infant Paris had been killed and the picture of old parents bereft of their children becomes clear at once when Menelaos arrives threatening to murder Andromache's child, whom he has in his control (309–10):[27]

I am here, having taken your child, whom you sent out
To another house for safety, behind my daughter's back.

The threat to Andromache's child, first mentioned by the Nurse (68ff) and obliquely repeated by Hermione (264), now is realised on stage. By using the Paris story in the ode followed by this entrance, Euripides juxtaposes two images — one past, one present; one of an infanticide that should have taken place and did not, the other that should not occur, but seems as if it will. The two images share the further similarity that both children were sent out of the house: Paris to be exposed but discovered by a well-intentioned shepherd; Andromache's son to be saved, but found by Menelaos. This juxtaposition of image and action accentuates the confusion, reversals and injustices that Troy and its aftermath bring.

In *El.*, as mentioned above, the pattern is reversed. Instead of a scene depicted in an ode and followed by a kindred action on stage, we find the stasimon describing a scene that has its stage counterpart before the song.[28] After Orestes and Elektra enjoy their recognition, and they and the Pedagogue plot the murders, the chorus relates the beginning of the Atreidae's woes — the fight over the golden lamb. The golden lamb, explains the chorus, was the sign of kingship, sent from the gods and conveyed by Pan to Atreus. The emphasis on the lamb is clear from the strophic repetition of 'golden lamb' (705) and 'golden lamb' (718).[29] In the previous scene the old Pedagogue, at Elektra's command (413ff), brought a lamb on stage when he entered at 487.[30] This Pedagogue also recognised Orestes, despite Elektra's opposition, and took the lead in plotting to restore Orestes to his throne. Like Pan in the myth (let us observe that the old man also dwells in the fields — see 410ff), he, too, in a sense, is a purveyor of kingship, with, moreover, greater success.

> As the lamb was the symbol of kingship three generations ago, so it remains the same symbol in the present event ... The style and context of the stasimon thrill the audience with a fresh discovery that the scene visually enacted a minute ago was not in reality Euripides' strange invention, but a theatrical image projected and repeated from the older myth of the Pelopidae.[31]

In the other cases, where the ode has preceded the parallel entrance, the relevant image came at or near the end of the song; here, where the stage action has come first, the ode begins with the parallel image.

A similar example of a mytho-historical backdrop to contrast with a following entrance is found in *Her.* A household servant emerges from the bloodshed and reports the barbarous deeds of Herakles (910ff). After this report confirming Lyssa's actions, the chorus sings that these murders surpass those of the Danaids and that of Prokne (1016ff). Then at 1028ff, they announce the 'entrance' of Herakles and the victims, as the *ekkyklema* is rolled out. In this case, however, in contrast to the others, the detailed messenger speech has already described the action that the 'entrance' reveals, and the effect of the juxtaposition is not the same.

Strikingly in the plays of Aischylos and Sophokles no true parallel can be found for the juxtaposition of image and action. The closest one is in *Ag.*, where the carpet-scene reflects in action themes that have been stated already and will be repeated throughout the trilogy. This stage action, however, differs from the ones we have looked at in Euripides in that it is not part of an entrance and, more important, refers to no specific image in the preceding lyric.

Effective Juxtaposition

Frequently an entrance after a lyric is not surprising, nor does it offer a vivid visual counterpart to the lyric, but the juxtaposition of entrance (or exit) and song is noteworthy. The poet uses this type of juxtaposition at the key moments of the beginnings and closings of acts to suggest a contrast or association important to the play.

Despite his wife's death, Admetos persuades a reluctant Herakles to be his guest (*xénos*) in *Alk.* After Herakles enters the house, Admetos defends his position to the chorus, explaining the importance he places on *xenia*. Four times from 550–67 he uses a form of *xénos* (three times in verse — final position), once the rare compound *echthróxenos* ('guest-hating'), and his parting words are (566–7):

> And my house does not know how
> To thrust away or to dishonour guests.

The chorus echoes the noble qualities of Admetos' house in the stasimon's opening address (568):

> Receiving-many-guests and always generous house of this man.
> (*ô polúxeinos kaì eleútheros andròs aeí pot' oîkos*)

In fact, the word *xénos* verbally frames this scene in which we witness Admetos' extreme form of *xenia*: *xénoi* is the initial word of Herakles' opening address (476) and *xénous* the final one of Admetos' closing speech (567). The ode also looks forward. Admetos leads out the funeral procession after the ode, and

Pheres' entrance is announced by the chorus. The contrast between the *xenia* of Admetos and Herakles and the hatred of father and son is sharpened by Pheres' entrance so soon after the ode, especially when in his first words to his father, Admetos excludes him from his friendship (630):

> Nor do I count you among my friends[32]

Before Jason's first entrance in *Med.* the chorus decries the present situation: justice and the faith established by oaths to the gods are gone (410ff); women have songs of infamy only because Apollo gave men the gift of song (421/ff). In the second strophic pair the chorus turns specifically to Medeia's situation ('And you ...', 431) and concludes with these lines (439–45):

> Gone is the charm of oaths, and no longer does a sense of
>   shame
> Remain in great Hellas — it has flown to the heavens.
> And you, unfortunate one, do not have your father's house
> As a refuge from these troubles.
> Another queen has taken your bed
> And rules in your house.

Directly following these words, Jason, who caused Medeia to forsake her home, who broke his oaths to the gods and replaced Medeia with a new bride, a prime example of the lack of justice and reverence, arrives for his first confrontation with Medeia. The song about the evil doings of men (see 426ff), which this play in part represents, now has its subject on stage. The ode proves in part ironic since, although the play clearly demonstrates the broken faith of Jason, Medeia's final brutal acts undercut the choral claim of women's undeserved reputation.

Immediately before Artemis appears at *Hipp.* 1283 the chorus, impressed by the destructive force of Kypris as related in the messenger's speech, proclaims the power of the goddess in a brief lyric (1268–82). At the end of the song they address the goddess, as they had at the beginning (1280–2):

> And you alone, Kypris, rule
> In royal power over all these.

Artemis, not Kypris, then appears in an attempt to reconcile the father and son that Aphrodite had separated. These two goddesses are opposed throughout the play. In fact, their appearances are mirror images that frame the drama. Aphrodite enters at the beginning and delivers the prologue, predicting Hippolytos' death and setting the play in motion, while Artemis appears towards the end and helps to bring the play to its conclusion. A further parallel is seen in the contrast made at Aphrodite's exit. Her departure is followed by the entrance of Hippolytos urging his companions to hymn Artemis (58ff). Artemis is preceded by a song to Aphrodite, Aphrodite followed by one to Artemis.

In *Her.* the entering choristers sing a brief triadic ode (107–37), emphasising their debilitating old age and their sympathies with the suppliants. In the epode they turn to the children, using the deictic pronoun *haide* at 131, and they remark on their physical resemblance to Herakles and the loss that their death will be to Hellas. Lykos enters (140) and demands why they seek to prolong their life (143). The fear expressed in the chorus' closing words is now palpable with the murderer's arrival, and the juxtaposition brings the threat to the family into sharper focus.

In the second stasimon of *Tro.* (799–859) the chorus complains that the gods have abandoned Troy.[33] Twice it has been sacked, and, although two Trojans have had divine lovers, this has won no favour. The second strophic pair is concerned with Ganymede's affair with Zeus and Tithonos' with Eos. The ode summarises the events with these words (858–9):

Troy's love charms over the gods are gone.

Menelaos then enters with an exclamation to the sunlight (860–1):

O this beautiful-shining brightness of the sun,
In which I will take my wife prisoner.

The emphatic address to the light of the sun recalls the description of Eos in antistrophe b ('light of white-winged Day').[34] The entrance is linked to the ode by more than verbal echoes. The war was fought to win back Menelaos' unfaithful wife; he reminds us of the senseless destruction of Troy that the ode relates. Secondly, can it be chance that following two strophes relating erotic affairs that might have saved Troy but did not, Menelaos arrives for his wife, whose affair with Paris caused the destruction, destruction which the gods did not prevent?

In *Hel.*, when Menelaos is rumoured to be dead, Helen takes the chorus' advice and approaches Theonoe to find out whether this is true. Before her exit, she laments the fate of Troy, compares her lot to that of Kallisto[35] and Merops' wife, and at the song's end returns to the destructive force of her beauty; it has destroyed Trojans and Greeks (383–5):

> My form
> Destroyed, destroyed the citadel of Troy
> And the perished Achaians.

Helen exits with the chorus, and Menelaos, a living, not a dead, Achaian and the one Helen is looking for, enters, wishing in a rather elaborate fashion that he had never been born. In a drama that explores the boundaries of truth and seeming and in which later are planned false funeral rites for Menelaos, this juxtaposition at Menelaos' first entrance is quite appropriate.

Immediately before Polyneikes enters in *Phoin.*, the chorus concludes the *parodos* (258–60):

> This is not an unjust
> Contest he rushes into, with an army,
> He who comes after his patrimony.

His subsequent entrance is not announced in these words. Although the lines do not describe Polyneikes (the chorus, as is evident from 286–7, does not even know who is approaching[36]) the juxtaposition is striking, both helping to link song to action and causing his entrance to be interpreted in the light of the words that still ring in the ears.

In *Bakch.* the band of maenads enters and hymns their god (64–169), describing the myth and the ritual of their cult. They present a picture of frenzied dancing and ecstasy, and the song's final image is the lively movement of a foal (165–9):

> With joy,
> Then, like a foal with its grazing mother,
> She moves with swift leaps, the bacchant.

The character who enters now is neither foal-like nor maenadic, but an old man — Teiresias. 'The cue is "Bacchanal" (169) — foal-like and nimble; the entry is that of a figure, wearing a Bacchic costume indeed, but male and old and blind.'[37] Although it is true that here uniquely Teiresias is not escorted onto the stage, and he and Kadmos feel young again (188–90), both of them are still old men (186, 193, 365) and wear masks that portray them as such. A verbal echo between the two entrances strengthens the contrast between the maenads and the old Teiresias (68–9):

> Who is on the road? Who is on the road? Who
> Is in the palace?

This is the chorus' first question when they enter. Teiresias' opening words ('Who is at the gates?', 170) remind us of the chorus' entrance.[38] Teiresias' situation — an old man trying to be young again under the god's influence (the chief source of the mild humour of this scene) — is effectively emphasised by the link of song and entrance.

The third stasimon of this play (862–911) responds to what has preceded and prepares for what follows. In the final line of the previous scene Dionysos describes himself as 'most terrible and most gentle to men' (861). The ode depicts both aspects of the divinity, the strophe relating the bliss of the god, the antistrophe his vengeance. The epode is a priamel[39] in which the chorus proclaims the blessedness of being *eudaimōn* day by day, concluding (910–11):

> And he whose life day by day is
> Happy, him I call blessed.

Dionysos enters, calling forth Pentheus, whose principles are antithetical to the new god and the chorus' credo, and who, the god has predicted and the ode suggested, will soon be punished.

2. Verbal Links

Announcements in lyric structures are rare.[40] The clear instances are found in *Alk.* and *Ion*, where Alkestis and Kreousa respectively are announced. There are noteworthy similarities between these two announcements: both occur at the end of a mimetic[41] song, the *parodos* in each play (*Alk.* 233ff and *Ion* 237); the context for both is dialogue (of members of the chorus in *Alk.*[42] and of the chorus and Ion in *Ion*); both are delivered by parties interested in the newcomer (the chorus and Ion respectively). Lyrics are also used to announce two 'entrances' in *Her.*: the *ekkyklema* scene at 1028ff and indirectly Herakles' waking at 1081ff, although the latter is not properly speaking an entrance announcement.[43]

We should not expect to find announcements in act-dividing songs. The basic pattern of song followed by entrance makes unnecessary, we have seen, an announcement at this juncture (except for 'moving tableaux') and songs, especially reflective ones, operate in a different mode from the dialogue and preclude almost entirely contact between the chorus and an entering character during the song.[44] But the poet can establish verbal links between the ends of lyrics and the scenes that start with the following entrances. Some involve the direct address or specific mention of the character who then arrives; others, verbal echoes between the conclusion of a lyric and the opening words of the next character (or the concluding dialogue picked up by the lyric).

Direct Address, Specific Mention

Euripides frequently uses direct address in his lyrics.[45] Often the person addressed is already on stage (e.g. Medeia at *Med.* 431ff) or has just departed (e.g. Peleus at *And.* 789ff). It is most exceptional for the character addressed to then arrive on stage, a 'talk of the devil' entrance.

The ending of *Hel.*'s second stasimon (1301–68) is extremely corrupt,[46] but it is clear at least that the chorus addresses Helen in the final stanza and refers to her with the second-person verb in the final line of the song (*éucheis*, 1368). Helen then enters to begin the next scene. Much debate has attended the dramatic relevance of the ode and the nature of Helen's 'offence';[47] I want only to suggest that a possible reason for the rare juxtaposition of a lyric address and the entrance of the addressed character is to strengthen the connection between the song and the action.[48]

Another character enters on the heels of being addressed in a lyric: Thetis in *And.* Peleus and the chorus lament in a mimetic song over Neoptolemos' corpse after it is brought in. At this point in the play it would not be highly unusual for a god, especially one who has been visually prominent throughout, to appear, explaining how recent events fit into a larger scheme. Thetis does appear, but atypically her appearance is preceded by Peleus' pathetic cry to his spouse (1224–5):

And you, daughter of Nereus, haunting gloomy caves,
You will see me falling, all ruined.

Thetis does not say that she comes in response to Peleus, but that is the effect of the juxtaposition.[49]

Other links do not involve an address to the character who then arrives, but the mention of the character at the end of the song followed by his entrance serves as a bridge between song and action. Again, the mention of the character who then enters does not imply contact between the chorus and the entering character.

When Medeia sends her children, bearing lethal gifts, to Jason's new wife (*Med.* 974ff), the chorus realises that this ensures the children's death. Their brief ode[50] begins (976–7):

Now no longer do I have hopes of the children's lives,
No longer; for already they walk towards murder.

At the end of this song they address Medeia, who, they say, will kill her children (996–9):

Next I lament your grief, wretched mother of children,
You who will murder them,
Because of a bridal bed.

The Pedagogue then enters with the children, exclaiming words of happiness (1002–4):

Lady, these children of yours are freed from the threat of exile.
The royal bride gladly received the gifts
In her hands. There the children are safe.

The Pedagogue's naïve and ironic words, juxtaposed to the end of the song, heighten the pathos of the children's lot; the audience is well aware of their grim ambiguity: not exile, but death now awaits the children.

The chorus and Elektra share the *parodos* in *El.* The latter sings the final section (198–212), lamenting her father's murder and her brother's and her own plight, and condemning Klytaimestra's life with a new husband. Her despair is great since not only does her father's murder go unpunished, while her mother shares a bed with Aigisthas, but Orestes, who might provide the aid she dearly needs, is, she thinks, wandering in a foreign land. Her description of her brother as an exile (202–5) is ironic since the audience already has seen him appear and go into hiding on stage, not very far from where Elektra is standing. Having heard what he desired, Orestes (after a two-line choral buffer, 213–14) emerges from hiding to his sister's shock. The audience has known Orestes' whereabouts all along, and the ironic mention of him near the end of the song and shortly before his appearance produces both greater expectation of his appearance and a stronger link between the song and the following scene.

Verbal Echoes

Verbal echoes at the juncture of entrance (or exit) and song can serve as links between the lyric and spoken parts of the dramas. For example, as already observed, in *Alk.* the key thematic word *xénos*, heard frequently at the end of the Herakles-Admetos scene is then echoed in the opening of the second stasimon, while the final stanza of the second stasimon of *Med.* repeats emphatically *philos*, which Aigeus' first words upon entering pick up. The five cases considered below have verbal echoes as a linking element. Not all involve a word as thematically important to the play as *xénos* in *Alk.* or *philos* in *Med.*, but all the echoes do serve as bridges between song and dialogue and several highlight an important point. Three of these cases connect the song to the preceding action, while two look forward. All but the first example from *Ion* contain a proper name.

In the first stasimon of *Hipp.* the chorus prays to avoid the devastating power of love and the formidable shafts of Aphrodite (525ff):

> Love, Love, you who shed desire
> On the eyes, bringing sweet pleasure
> To the soul on whom you make your attack,
> May you never appear with evil intent
> Nor come out of measure.
> For neither of fire nor of the stars does the shaft surpass

That of Aphrodite, which Eros, Zeus' son, hurls from his hands.

The song responds to Phaidra's condition and revelation in the previous scene, but, more specifically, it follows directly after the Nurse, about to exit, has invoked Aphrodite as her ally (522–3):[51]

> Only, may you, mistress Kypris of the Sea,
> Be my ally.

Aphrodite is, as the audience already knows and the next scene reveals, a too powerful and destructive ally, a fact that the verbal echo puts into sharp relief.

There seems to be a verbal connection between the end of Hermes' prologue speech and Ion's entering monody in *Ion*. Hermes explains why he is exiting (78–80):

> For I see Loxias' son coming forth,
> This one, so he can make the temple's gateway bright (*lamprá*)
> With laurel branches.

Brightness (*lamprá*) pervades Ion's opening address to the sun, as a form of *lamp-* appears three times (82–3; 86–7):[52]

> Here are the bright (*lamprá*) four-horsed chariots;
> Already Helios shines (*lámpei*) down on the earth.

> And the untrodden peaks of Parnassos
> Struck by the light (*katalampómenai*)

Euripides' fondness for verbal repetitions is well known.[53] Here the repeated emphasis on brightness not only helps to connect prologue to monody, but also might suggest Apollo in his role of sun god (see Chapter 5).

Despite textual problems it is evident that *Ion*'s second stasimon ends, after a wish for Ion's death, with a reminder of the legitimate line to the throne — that of Erechtheus. The song concludes (721ff):

> For a city in troubled times might have an excuse
> ... foreign influx
> ....

... the ruler of old
King Erechtheus.[54]

Kreousa then enters with the old family servant and calls to him with the name of her race's founder ('Old man, tutor of Erechtheus, my late father', 725–6), echoing the last words of the song and highlighting the ironic conflict between Kreousa and Ion which will result in the plotting against his life in this scene.

Helen ends the long scene before the first stasimon in *Hel.* with a prayer to Hera and Aphrodite that Menelaos and she may escape (1093ff). These two goddesses are not ignored in the following stasimon; the names are prominently placed at the final position of strophe and antistrophe, and since both words are in the genitive case, they also rhyme.[55] This striking association recalls Helen's prayer before her exit.

In the first stasimon of *Or.* the chorus sings about the Eumenides and the problems of the house of Tantalos. The general statement on the mutability of human fortune (340) is proved *a fortiori* by the example of this house: for what house, they rhetorically ask, is more worthy of reverence (345–7):

> For yet what house should I reverence
> Before the one from divine unions,
> The one from Tantalos?

Menelaos' entrance (discussed above in Chapter 2) is then announced in anapests (348–51):

> And here comes the king,
> Lord Menelaos, with much splendour,
> So that it is plain to see
> That he is from the line of Tantalos.

The verbal echo, linking song to entrance, heightens the contrast between the promise and the fulfilment of Menelaos' arrival and the double reference to the house's Lydian ancestor underlines the pompous and luxurious entrance.

3. Prayers and Predictions

Many odes contain a prayer or a prediction which is answered (positively or negatively) in the next entrance. Often a messenger supplies the answer to the prayer or prediction with his report; the connection is thus somewhat less sharp since the event is once removed, but it is not insignificant. This section surveys the links between lyrics containing prayers or predictions and the following entrance.

Prayers

At *Hkld.* 747 Iolaos and his companions exit to join the battle against the Argive forces, and the chorus prays for the army's success (748–83). A messenger arrives at the end of the song, announcing the good news of Athenian victory. Similarly at *Hik.* 598ff the chorus, filled with fear, prays at the ode's end for the victory of Theseus in his efforts to win burial for the bodies. This victory is announced in the following entrance of a messenger (634). Before Menelaos departs with Helen at *Hel.* 1450, he prays to Zeus for a successful journey home.[56] The chorus then picks up this wish and prays that Menelaos, Helen and they themselves may fly home (1451–1511). They turn to the Dioskouroi in the second antistrophe and ask that they give the couple safe escort and save Helen's name. A messenger arrives directly after this prayer and announces the fulfilment of the first part of the prayer to the Dioskouroi; the twins themselves must appear to effect the second part (1642ff).

The prayer to Dionysos in the epode of *Bakch.* 519–75 is answered by no messenger. With their leader imprisoned, the maenads sing to Dirke and assert their belief in Dionysos. The song concludes in a kletic hymn to Dionysos:[57] he will come, the chorus proclaims. As if in answer to their prayer,[58] Dionysos shouts from off-stage and announces his identity (576ff).[59]

Prayers are not always answered affirmatively. At *Ion* 1048ff, e.g., the chorus prays to Einodia that Kreousa's and the Pedagogue's plans to murder the apparent usurper Ion may be successful, and they conclude with a strong condemnation of Xouthos. Their plea is to no avail, however, as we discover with the servant's entrance (1106) and report of the failed assassination and his search for Kreousa.

At other times a prayer is not so much answered negatively as followed by something antithetical to this wish. Earlier in *Ion*, after the first episode reveals Kreousa's situation, the chorus prays that the race of Erechtheus (Kreousa's family) may have a son (468–71):

> Pray, maiden goddesses,
> That Erechtheus' race of old
> With clear oracles
> May meet with children after a long time.

At the end of the song they tell the tale of the girl exposing her child. The audience's attention is on Kreousa, her abandoned son, and her hope for another, when Ion who, of course, is her son, enters, looking for Xouthos. The latter arrives almost immediately, and we witness not Kreousa finding her child, but Xouthos discovering 'his'. ('Child, greetings!', 517, are the proud father's first words when he enters.) The 'answer' to the chorus' prayer produces a strong contrast between ode and entrance, and points to the conflict to be played out in the drama.

After Helen exits with Menelaos in *Tro.*, the chorus (1060–1117) criticises Zeus for destroying Troy, laments its own fate, and, in the final stanza, wishes[60] that Menelaos and Helen never reach home. The following entrance reveals no such thing, but rather the dead Astyanax. *IT* contains a similar sequence. At the end (439ff) of the first stasimon the chorus wishes that Iphigeneia's prayers that Helen may come and pay the penalty by being sacrificed to Artemis may come true. Orestes and Pylades, not Helen, then are announced after the ode as the new sacrifice to the goddess (456–8):

> But here these two come,
> Their hands bound with chains,
> The latest sacrifice to the goddess.

Predictions

We also find in lyrics predictions of events, the success of which is confirmed in the subsequent entrance. In three cases (*Hek.* 1024ff, *Her.* 734ff, and *El.* 1147ff) the choral song follows the exit of an unsuspecting victim (Polymestor, Lykos, and Klytaimestra respectively) into the *skene*, where, the chorus and audience well know, someone lies in ambush. The sequence of events follows a similar pattern in all three plays: exit into the *skene*; words at the back directly or indirectly predicting the murder;[61] a brief choral lyric also predicting the murder; cries from within;[62] an entrance from the *skene* confirming the success of the predictions. In *Antiope* (fr. 48) Euripides presents a variation of this pattern. Amphion and Zethos plot the death of Lykos on stage and exit into the *skene* to prepare the murder. Lykos then enters and is led into the *skene* by the herdsman, and the chorus (in a few trimeters and dochmiacs) foretells Lykos' death.[63] The cries from within, however, do not indicate success and Hermes appears suddenly to stop the murder.[64]

The prediction and confirmation of fraternal murder in *Phoin.* follows a different pattern. No plotting is involved and the double fratricide occurs not in the *skene*, but off-stage. The chorus' prediction in the fourth stasimon (1284ff) is preceded by an earlier messenger's reluctant admission (1217ff) that the brothers are preparing to fight each other. A messenger confirms their deaths, but not immediately. As the text stands,[65] Kreon's entrance intervenes before the messenger arrives with the news.

All of these cases differ from *Med.* 976ff (described above) where the chorus sings that Medeia will kill the children, and the children then enter. The children, unlike the others, are seen alive after the prediction; their return after the prediction increases the tension during Medeia's emotional debate over her final decision to kill them, a debate that is still to be played out on stage.

Two odes do not so much predict future bloodshed as describe vividly, almost clairvoyantly, the events that are then confirmed.[66] When in *Bakch.* Dionysos is about to exit with the 'bacchant' Pentheus, he calls to Agave that he is leading him into the maenads' hands (973ff), and the chorus then sings an ode that both urges on the action and envisions it. They call to the hounds of Lyssa to go to the hills and goad the maenads against Pentheus (977ff), and their refrain (991–6 = 1011–16) calls on *dike* to slay him; they even relate the questions that they imagine Agave will ask about this intruder, her son (985ff):[67]

Who is this seeker of Kadmeian mountain-dancers,
This one who came to the mountains,
Came to the mountains, bacchants? Who gave him birth?
For he is not from the blood of women,
But his race is from some lion
Or of Libyan Gorgons.

Pentheus' death is obliquely predicted by Dionysos as they depart (971ff) (and directly by the god earlier, 857ff), urged on and imagined in the lyric, and then confirmed with the messenger scene (1024ff), and finally witnessed in Agave's display of his severed head (1168ff) and Kadmos' return with the body (1216ff).

An equally vivid 'visionary' ode is the second stasimon of *Hipp.* After Phaidra's ominous departure from the stage (731), the chorus wishes to escape from the present crisis. The song ends not with an expression of fear that Phaidra will kill herself (she said that she would do that, 715ff), but with a clairvoyant picture of what will happen inside the palace (769–72):

> And overwhelmed by this hard misfortune,
> She will attach from the beams of her wedding chamber
> A suspended noose, fitting it to her white neck.

Their vision is confirmed immediately when the Nurse calls from within for their help since Phaidra has hanged herself (776–7) and, after Theseus' arrival, the suicide is visually revealed when the corpse is rolled out on the *ekkyklema* (811ff).

Notes

1. This is the implication of *Poetics* 1456a 25ff.
2. For this interpretation of the passage, see G. Else, *Aristotle's Poetics: The Argument* (Cambridge, Mass. 1957), 551–60, and D.W. Lucas, *Aristotle: Poetics* (Oxford 1968), 193–4.
3. On the influence of the 'new music' on Euripidean lyrics, see Kranz, 38ff. Among recent works dealing with the dramatic relevance of his odes, see H. Neitzel, *Die dramatische Funktion der Chorlieder in den Tragödien des Euripides* (Diss. Hamburg 1967) and H. Parry, *The Lyric Poems of Greek Tragedy* (Toronto and Sarasota 1978).
4. Schmid-Stählin, I. 3, 785.
5. For the present discussion the distinction between strophic and astrophic is irrelevant.
6. The inner movement of the songs, although not our main concern, is given some attention in passing.
7. We should point out that, although these two entrances possess no special link to the preceding ode, the songs do connect in different ways to the previous scenes. In *Hik.* the choral plea for the city to defend them *qua* mothers (377) parallels the display of filial piety just shown by Theseus. As we point out below, there are verbal links between Helen's exit and the subsequent song.
8. Also not discussed are songs linked to the preceding action by a specific injunction to the chorus to sing, as at, e.g., *Tro.* 143ff, *Bakch.* 55ff.
9. Kranz, in his discussion of odes of false preparation (213ff), mentions *Med.*

627ff and *Her.* 763ff, only to dismiss them. Sophokles alone, he thought, had this type of choral ode. W. Helg, *Das Chorlied der griechischen Tragödie in seinem Verhältnis zur Handlung* (Diss. Zürich, Oberwintherthur 1950), omits Euripides from his section on songs *parà prosdokían.* J. Rode, 'Das Chorlied' in W. Jens (ed.), *Die Bauformen der griechischen tragödie* (Munich 1971) 108, includes *Alk.* 962ff, *Her.* 348ff, *Her.* 763ff, *Bakch.* 519ff among his examples.

10. For the progression from the general statement to the specific example in this and other lyrics, see Kranz, 217ff.

11. For a recent discussion of life and death in *Alk.*, see J. Gregory, 'Euripides' *Alcestis*', *Hermes* 107 (1979), 259–70.

12. See H. Parry, 'The Second Stasimon of Euripides's *Heracles* (637–700)', *AJP* 86 (1965), 363–74.

13. Parry, above n. 3, 161–2, argues that in the light of what he feels are ambiguities earlier in the ode the doubt is even greater; but see below, Chapter 5 n. 27.

14. Kranz discusses this type of ode, 211–13.

15. See Chapter 2 n. 15.

16. On the difference in the motivation for the entrance and exit in these two plays, see Bond (ed.), *Her.*, 178.

17. Kranz, 212, details these similarities.

18. For words at a departing character's back, see Chapter 3 n. 7.

19. In passing it may be noted that the same actor probably played both roles.

20. Excluded from discussion is the sequence we find at *El.* 1147ff, e.g., of a lyric predicting the soon-to-occur murder and the following 'entrance' of the corpse on the *ekkyklema.* The sight of the corpse only confirms the prediction of murder; it does not recreate in some way an image in the song. This and similar scenes are discussed later in this chapter.

21. Polydoros' ghost had, of course, foretold in the prologue that the corpse would be discovered on the shore by a slave (47–48).

22. In fact, Polymestor's butchery and betrayal of friendship are not known before Euripides' play. In the *Iliad* Achilleus ends Polydoros' life (20, 407ff), and Laothoë, not Hekabe, is his mother (21, 84ff.). On the possibility that Euripides employed a local legend, see H. Weil (ed.), *Sept tragédies d'Euripide*[2] (Paris 1913) in his introduction to the play, 207.

23. See, e.g., D. Conacher, *Euripidean Drama: Myth, Theme and Structure* (Toronto 1967), 155–65. And see Friedrich, above, Chapter 3 n. 17.

24. See P. Arnott, *Greek Scenic Conventions* (Oxford 1962), 116, for this implicit contrast.

25. D. Page (ed.), *ad loc.*, maintains that the version given by Euripides here 'must have been current before Eur.'s allusion to it here: the poet cannot have introduced even so slight an innovation in a passing reference intended as a parallel.' If Page is correct, it is then noteworthy that this version is so uncommon that it is mentioned elsewhere only by Nymphodorus Syracusianus (*FGrH* 572, F18). For a recent treatment of Euripides' use of the Ino story in this play, see S.P. Mills, 'The Sorrows of Medea', *CP* 75 (1980), 289–96.

26. See Kranz, 216.

27. Is he holding the child as he speaks, making the threat more vivid? Unfortunately there is nothing in the text to prove it, or in the iconographic evidence to suggest it.

28. See M. Kubo, 'The Norm of Myth: Euripides' *Electra*', *HSCP* 71 (1966) 15–31, for a detailed account of the similarities between the stage action and the ode. My discussion is owed to this article.

29. Diggle correctly prints 705 with Heath's conjecture.

30. He does not explicitly refer to the animal he brings on stage with him as a

lamb, but the language of 494—5 suggests that it is. Iconography does not assist us here since nowhere do we find Orestes' Pedagogue carrying a sacrificial victim on stage. Similarly, other literary versions make no mention of a lamb or other animal brought by the Pedagogue. Since Euripides seems to have innovated also in the setting of this play and the character of the farmer, the apparent uniqueness of the lamb should cause no surprise. Clearly Euripides adds the detail of the lamb in order to make stronger the connection between past and present.

31. Kubo, above n. 28, 20.

32. We should add that there is an implicit contrast between the reverence (*aidōs*) Admetos shows in his *xenia* towards Herakles and the lack of it he reveals to his father, who also acts with utter shamelessness in the following scene. This is especially pointed after the chorus claims that Admetos' *aidōs* is the result of his noble heritage (*tò eugenés*) (600—1).

33. A good treatment of this ode is A.P. Burnett, '*Trojan Women* and the Ganymede Ode' *YCS* 25 (1977), 291—316.

34. Parry, above n. 3, 179, makes a similar suggestion.

35. See Kannicht and Dale (eds.), *ad loc.*, for the problems surrounding these lines.

36. See Mastronarde, 100, and 100 n. 14, for the interpretation of 258—60.

37. R.P. Winnington-Ingram, *Euripides and Dionysus* (Cambridge 1948), 40.

38. This is not an unusual question in tragedy (see, e.g., Roux (ed.), *ad loc.*). But after the emphatic triple *tis* of the *parodos*, I think that the connection between the two is likely.

39. See Dodds (ed.), 190, for the progression of thought in this epode.

40. On this topic see Taplin, 173—4, and Mastronarde, 100—1.

41. On the differences between 'mimetic' and 'reflective' songs, see Rode, above n. 9, 90—9. Mastronarde, 101, also points to the mimetic nature of these songs.

42. See Dale (ed.), 67—8, on the possibilities of distribution and Prinz-Wecklein (eds.), for further suggestions.

43. The announcement at *Hik.* 794ff should also be mentioned here; it falls *within* a lyric structure, but is not in a lyric metre. On this and examples in the other two tragedians, see Taplin, 174. The announcement of the divine apparition at *Her.* 815ff is in lyric iambs, but not in a lyric structure.

44. See, e.g., the comments of Hourmouziades, 140—1. We should also emphasise that an address in a lyric does not imply contact or the desire to establish contact; see Mastronarde, 98ff.

45. Often to shift the song's movement; see Kranz, 206ff.

46. See Kannicht and Dale (eds.), *ad loc.*

47. See recently Parry, above n. 3, 180—5.

48. A parallel for the situation in *Hel.* might be found in *And.*, but two problems make it uncertain. To whom does the 'you' at the end of the fourth stasimon refer (1041)? If it refers to Andromache (the strongest case for Hermione is made by W. Steidle, *Studien zum antiken Drama* (Munich 1968), 118—21), does she then appear with Peleus at 1047? As Stevens (ed.), *ad loc.*, concludes, after a survey of the evidence, 'None of the points is conclusive,' See also Mastronarde, 99—101.

49. 'On this cue, Thetis prepares to enter,' remarks Stevens (ed.), *ad loc.*

50. K. Aichele, *Die Epeisodien der griechischen Tragödie* (Diss. Tübingen 1966) 18, provides the statistics to show that the fourth and fifth stasima tend to be the briefest, producing less of a break in the action as the play draws near to its conclusion.

51. For prayers upon exit, see Schadewaldt, *Monolog und Selbstgespräch: Untersuchungen zur Formgeschichte der griechischen Tragödie*, Neue Philologische Untersuchungen 2 (Berlin 1926), 75 and n. 3 and 101—4.

52. Some critics have been bothered by this repetition. Musgrave conjectured *kámptei* for *lámpei*, and this was accepted by Prinz-Wecklein and called 'attractive' by Owen (ed.), *ad loc.* Diggle keeps the *lámpei* of the mss.

53. He is best known for the successive repetition of words, of which practice his earliest critic was Aristophanes (see; e.g., *Frogs* 1336 and 1352ff). Euripides also repeated words and phrases with only a short interval between them, usually with no special purpose (see Schmid-Stählin, I. 3, 795); the effect here I suggest in the text.

54. A.P. Burnett (trans.), *Ion* (Englewood Cliffs, N.J. 1970), 75, also comments on the attention given to Erechtheus at the end of the song ('the last note struck'), but she does not observe the verbal connection to the following entrance.

55. Kannicht (ed.), 286, also comments on the emphatic placement of the names (a feature of choral lyric) and the connection between the prayer and the song.

56. Theoklymenos has probably already departed; see Kannicht (ed.), 373, and Dale (ed.), 156.

57. See Kranz, 234—5.

58. Kranz, 235, Dodds (ed.), *ad loc.*, and Roux (ed.), *ad loc.*, are among those who make the same comment.

59. The closest parallel in Greek tragedy to this 'answered' prayer is Aisch. *Eum.* 397, where Athene arrives in response to Orestes' call. See Taplin, 387—8, on this scene.

60. On the use of *eithe*, employed here, to mark a transition within a lyric, see Kranz, 250.

61. D. Bain, *Actors and Audience: A Study of Asides and Related Conventions in Greek Drama* (Oxford 1977), 34—5, distinguishes between Amphitryon's remarks as Lykos exits in *Her.* (726—8), which can be taken as a 'general threat', and the very explicit 'words at the back' delivered by Elektra in *El.* The difference informs us about the respective stagings of these scenes, but the audience has no more doubt about the significance of Amphitryon's words than it has about Elektra's. In any case, Amphitryon follows his 'general threat' with an explicit one (729ff).

62. See Hourmouziades, 88ff, for a discussion of these interior scenes.

63. On the text and supplements, see Kambitsis (ed.), *ad loc.*

64. A somewhat similar sequence of action is found in *Or.*, but there Hermione is led into the *skene*, not the intended victim, Helen (her daughter is only 'insurance' against failure to murder her), and Helen's cries from within are heard before Hermione's exit into the *skene*. The chorus does not predict the murder, but does claim that the nemesis from the gods has come to Helen (1361ff). The failure to murder Helen, one of many failed actions in the play (see above Chapter 3 n. 15) is reported by the addled Phrygian, whose entrance begins the next scene.

65. For the problems of the text, see Chapter 2 n. 55.

66. C Möller, *Vom Chorlied bei Euripides* (Diss. Göttingen, Bottrop 1933), 66, and Dodds (ed.), *Bakch.*, *ad loc.*, consider *Med.* 976ff as well as the two discussed below 'visionary' odes.

67. On recording direct speech within choral lyric, see Kranz, 259 and 314—15.

5 THREE PLAYS

1. Herakles

In his opening *rhesis* Amphitryon does not refer to his supplication at the altar until line 48. Thus readers of the text are ignorant of the setting until that point, but the audience is immediately aware of this setting, since they see Amphitryon and the others there at the play's beginning. Because no curtain unveils the tableau, the audience also sees the characters come on stage and assume their suppliant pose. This type of 'cancelled'[1] first entrance is not uncommon in tragedy; it permits at the opening of the play a tableau which the audience 'discovers' and by convention assumes to have been there for a certain length of time (not inconsiderable in this case; see 51–3). Significantly, we see Amphitryon, Megara and Herakles' children in this opening tableau; it suggests that they are immobile and passive — the altar is their only refuge. Amphitryon's *rhesis* verbally confirms and strengthens the visual suggestion of helplessness. Since Herakles has not returned from his final labour (in Hades) and the usurper Lykos has threatened to murder the family, they have taken refuge at the altar (22–41). Amphitryon himself can offer no defence: old age virtually excludes him from the ranks of men (41–2). They need someone to save them (54), since their friends are either incapable of providing aid or are not true friends after all: misfortune is the truest test of friendship (55–9).

Opening tableaux in Euripides, whether of suppliants or not (the others are *Hkld.*, *And.*, *Hik.*, *Tro.*, *Hel.*, *Or.*), always depict the helplessness and typically the isolation of the character(s) involved. Here the tableau, showing the family's plight, suggests the tension that is played out in the first part of the drama: Herakles' family needs someone to save them — who, if anyone, will be their saviour? Ironically, as it turns out, they are suppliants at an altar dedicated to Zeus the Saviour (48), an altar set up by Herakles himself (49–50). The family's special connection to Zeus, familiar from mythology and proudly emphasised in the play's opening lines, does not bring them any aid (as Amphitryon thinks it should; see 339ff), even when they supplicate at his altar.

Megara replies to Amphitryon's speech with despair and an acceptance of the inevitability of death (70ff), and Amphitryon concludes the scene with an exhortation to maintain hope, hope which even he will abandon in the next act. The chorus of old Theban men then enters, singing the *parodos*. In three other 'suppliant' plays (*Hkld., And., Hel.*) the chorus arrives with concern for the welfare of the characters on stage.[2] In *Her.* Euripides shows a chorus concerned with the suppliants' welfare, but he has them devote most of the *parodos* to a description of their own decrepit state. They are no more than words and dreams (111–12), they proclaim, and merely walking is an effort for them (118ff). By emphasising their debilitated condition, Euripides underlines the family's helplessness. These men are well-intentioned towards the suppliants and eager to help (114), but as their belaboured entrance and song tell us, they cannot. Amphitryon was right: those who are the family's friends are unable to come to their rescue. Later in the play the choristers can offer only *words* in response to Lykos' threats despite their talk of action (252ff, 312ff).[3] Help, if it is to come, must come from another source.

We noted in Chapter Two the anomaly of the chorus' entrance (107) not being announced despite the presence of more than one person on stage. Might this breaking of the convention serve to emphasise the suppliants' isolation and passivity? They appear on stage at the play's beginning, and, needless to say, they do not exit before the chorus arrives. We expect from them an announcement of the chorus, but find none. The family appears static and incapable of even the simplest action.

The end of the *parodos* leads into the following scene. The deictic pronoun *haide* (131) marks a transition towards the more specific concern with the children, and the closing appeal to Hellas at the loss of the children (135–7) implicitly prepares us for Lykos' entrance. Although Lykos is not actually named in the *parodos*, the prologue scene makes clear who is going to rob Hellas of these children, and almost at once upon arrival (140) he asks the suppliants why they seek to prolong their life (143). The juxtaposition of song and entrance underscores the imminence of the murders. (The reason for the announcement (138–9) of an entrance directly following the strophic song was discussed in Chapter 2.) The entrance after the *parodos* is often reserved for an important or dominant character — e.g. Medeia in *Med.*, Phaidra in *Hipp.*, Kreousa in *Ion.*[4] Lykos, the threat depicted in the prologue scene and prepared for at the end of the *parodos*, enters, and the helpless family of Herakles is now confronted by their potential murderer. We have observed that an entering character usually initiates the action by speaking first when he enters, and Lykos is no exception in this regard, as he begins the conversation when he arrives. In fact, he begins by delivering a thirty-line speech.[5] Although this is not extremely unusual, it is not the normal pattern: generally an entering character establishes contact with those on stage by way of a dialogue, and then he might have a *rhesis. And.* provides a close parallel:[6] Andromache is a suppliant at an altar and, after the *parodos*, the persecutor, Hermione, arrives with threats. Hermione is aggressive and domineering, while Andromache, until she starts her reply, seems passive and powerless at the altar. In *Her.* not only do Lykos' words seem threatening, but the pattern of a long *rhesis* upon entrance also suggests his dominance.[7]

Although he loses the argument with Amphitryon, Lykos does not delay in carrying out his threats. He responds with actions, not words (238–9): he will burn them at the altar (242ff). The chorus of weak, old men can, we have noted, do nothing but verbally condemn Lykos. Fire is not needed, however, since Megara, faced with what she feels is the necessity of death (282ff) and sure that Herakles will not return from Hades (296ff), convinces Amphitryon of her decision to leave the altar and face death bravely. She does win from Lykos permission to enter the house in order to put on the proper garments for death (327ff).[8]

Lykos, claiming that he will return when the family has donned these garments, exits down one of the *parodoi* at 335. Megara bids the children to accompany her inside the house (336–8), while Amphitryon, before his departure, calls on Zeus and reproaches him for not aiding the family of his reputed son (339–47). This succession of three exits[9] has drawn the attention of no one, although it has only one close parallel in Greek tragedy — *Ion* 442ff, where Xouthos, Kreousa, and Ion leave the stage successively. What is the effect of the triple successive exits in *Her.*? A suppliant leaves the altar either when he has been saved or when he goes to his death.[10] Here the latter is the case (at least it seems to be) and the unusual exit pattern highlights this solemn moment. Secondly, as in *Ion*, the last one to exit, Amphitryon, has a brief soliloquy, in which he challenges Zeus and claims superiority as the mortal father of Herakles.[11] After the first two exits, the spotlight, as it were, falls on Amphitryon, and the questions he raises about divine justice and Herakles' paternity[12] — major themes of the play — receive greater emphasis. That it is Zeus' altar that they are abandoning gives Amphitryon's remarks added point.

The first stasimon (348–441) begins after Amphitryon exits into the *skene*. His closing comparison to Zeus as the father of Herakles is echoed in the first strophe, as the chorus is uncertain whether to call Herakles the son of Zeus or the son of Amphitryon (353–4).[13] A further, more subtle connection is perhaps found in the juxtaposition of the exit to don the new garments and the description in the second stanza of the first labour, Herakles killing the Nemean lion — and wearing its skin (359–63):

> First he rid Zeus' grove
> Of the lion,
> And putting the skin on his back
> He covered his blond head
> With the dread beast's tawny jaw.

The Nemean lion, the canonical first labour, not surprisingly is related first; the emphasis in the song, however, falls not on the struggle, but on the donning of the lion skin. Herakles put on the lion skin, and this skin made him invulnerable. (Although the invincibility of the skin is not referred to here, it was sufficiently well known from mythological tradition and choral poetry[14].) His father, wife and children have just departed to dress in robes that mean their death (although ultimately from a different and unexpected source). The connection between these robes and the lion skin is not, we have noted, explicitly made, only suggested by the juxtaposition. Attention is drawn, however, to these funereal garments both before the ode (329ff) and immediately afterwards (442–3).

The ode in its conclusion moves towards the present situation: after singing of Herakles' 'final' labour, the descent into Hades, from which he has not returned (425ff), the old men return in the last stanza to their own inability to defend the children (436–41):

> But if I had the strength of my youth
> And could wield the spear in battle,
> With my Theban comrades,
> I would champion the children.
> But as things are now, I lack my blessed youth.

The old men's inability to defend the children, caused by their lack of youth (emphatically stated by the placement of *hébōn* and *hébās* at verse-final position, 436, 441), prepares us for the following entrance. And when the family enters from the *skene*, it is the children who receive the first individual announcement (444–5).

The chorus announces in anapests this entrance of the children, Megara and Amphitryon directly after a strophic song (442–50). In Chapter 2 we observed that the entrance was one of several 'moving tableaux' in Euripides — a slow, stately or solemn entrance, in this case of those condemned to die. The announcement, unusual according to the basic pattern of entrance announcements, draws attention to the entrance and highlights the pathos of these innocent victims. Their suffering is also reflected in the tears of the chorus (449–50). The vivid description of the children and Megara also underscores their pathetic entrance (444–7):

> The children of once-great Herakles
> And his wife dragging behind her
> The children who cling to her feet . . .[15]

As suggested in Chapter 4, the scene following this ode and leading up to Herakles' arrival is, in a sense, an extension of the previous action, the final build-up to that entrance. We witness Megara's laments over the imminent murders and her wistful reminiscences of Herakles' (unfulfilled) promises to the children (451ff). Amphitryon issues his second challenge to Zeus and reflects on the uncertainties of life (497ff). (Note the repetition of *mátēn* in the two challenges to Zeus, twice in the first one (339–40) and once in the second (501).) The scene recreates their hapless situation, only now they are even closer to death as they appear in their funeral robes and no longer sit at Zeus' altar (still a visible stage property). Herakles is needed to save them, but, we have heard repeatedly throughout the first part of the drama, he is in Hades and cannot return.

The ode celebrating Herakles' labours makes it especially surprising that he appears, since, as Wilamowitz suggested,[16] the song is a type of *thrênos* in praise of the dead Herakles. The song thus embodies the tension that the playwright creates and plays with in the first third of the drama. Extolling Herakles' exploits, the chorus reminds us of how great a hero he was and (implicitly) how easily he could right the situation in Thebes, but the *thrênos* form tells us that he is dead. And the song emphatically ends with his 'final' labour (*pónōn teleután,* 427[17]); he remains in Hades. Herakles cannot return to save his family, yet at the same time the force of the drama seems to demand that he do just that.[18] This paradox animates the first part of the play, as Euripides manipulates the audience both to deny the possibility and to feel keenly the need of Herakles' arrival. The arrival that one should expect on the surface level is that of Lykos, who said that he would return as soon as the victims had put on their robes (334–5), and this expectation (the murderer's entrance is overdue) adds to the tension of the scene.

Before Amphitryon's speech that immediately precedes Herakles' entrance, Megara ends her reflections with a final despairing call to Herakles, concluding with a *tricolon crescendo* that rhetorically emphasises the family's sore need (494–5):

Help! Come! Appear to me even as a shadow!
For it would be enough even if you came as a dream.

Amphitryon's final prayer, directed to Zeus, bespeaks resignation (esp. 502) more than a request for help. Overturning this despair and as if in answer to Megara's prayer, Herakles does (finally) arrive, a surprising entrance at the critical moment, producing the first major turnabout of the play. We do not find a simple two- or three-line entrance announcement followed by Herakles' initiation of dialogue with those on stage; the potential dramatic force of the moment is exploited fully by Euripides.

'*éa*', Megara exclaims, when she thinks she spots Herakles entering from the *parodos.* She says it may be a dream (517–18), echoing her prayer that he come even as a dream; but finally she realises that it is, in fact, her husband and she bids the children to cling to his robes.[19] The gradual realisation that Herakles has suddenly appeared effectively displays her confusion, disbelief and joy at his appearance. Herakles enters, but he does not at first notice his family before him. His first words, appropriately for one returning home, are a greeting to home and hearth (523–4). Then he sees his family in their death robes and, upon making this contact, he cries out *éa* (reminding us of Megara's cry when she first saw him arriving?). Mastronarde has formulated a scheme for this type of Euripidean entrance pattern, which he calls 'partial vision': (1) comment of newcomer in isolation from contact; (2) visual contact *parodos*-to-stage (frequently marked, as here, by *éa* with comment out of contact); (3) initiation of dialogue. Both the atypical announcement and the use of 'partial vision' help to highlight the importance of the entrance and the emotion of the characters.

Reunited with his family and informed of Lykos' crimes, Herakles promises protection and revenge. At the end of the scene (636), Herakles, his children, wife and father exit into the *skene* together (not separately as the family did at the end of the previous act). Herakles describes how he and the children enter into the palace (631–2):

> Taking them by the hand I will lead these little boats
> And like a ship I will pull them in tow.

This description of the exit reminds us of the children's entrance at the beginning of the act. We recall that the chorus described the children's entrance with Megara in these words (445–47):

> And his wife dragging behind her
> The children who cling to her feet.

The chorus does not employ the nautical image, but *ephélkxō* (632) echoes *hélkousan* (446), and the descriptions of the entrance and exit are similar in other respects also. Tears accompany both entrance and exit: at the end of the announcement of the family (442–50), the chorus proclaims that it cannot hold back its tears (449–50) and Herakles tells the children to stop their tears as they all begin to exit (625). A comparison between entrance and exit, explicitly suggesting that they are 'mirror scenes', is made in fact by Herakles himself (622–4):

> But come, children, into your father's house.
> Fairer are your entrances into it
> Than your exits from it.

The entrance from the *skene* at the beginning of the scene seemed to mean the family's death and did not, while the exit which concludes the scene seems to indicate their safety and does not. The drama is only half-finished, and another and more surprising turnabout remains. 'Everyone loves his children,' (636) Herakles' final words as he exits, possess, as the audience will see, a very grim irony.

The famous hymn to Youth is sung in response to Herakles' return and rescue of his family. The previous song had been a *thrênos*, singing the praises of the (presumed) dead Herakles; this one functions as an encomium of the living and triumphant hero.[20] And it aids in the establishment of the victorious mood that will soon be shattered. The chorus concludes with emphatic praise of Herakles' *aretê*[21] (696–700):

> He is Zeus' son. Surpassing
> In excellence more than in birth,
> With much toil he made life
> Tranquil for mortals
> By destroying terrifying beasts.

This closing is connected to the following entrance. Lykos arrives as these words still ring in our ears. Following these words the tyrant, whose name, of course, means wolf, seems to be another beast whose terror Herakles will extinguish.[22] The ode, then, both extols Herakles' previous feats and leads into the next one.

Lykos and Amphitryon arrive almost simultaneously after the stasimon, the former appearing on stage only shortly before the latter emerges from the *skene*.[23] Lykos is informed that the family has taken refuge at the hearth within, and he is easily duped into entering the house, where, the audience well knows, Herakles lies in ambush. In his brief exchange with Lykos, Amphitryon employs ambiguous and occasionally false words; once Lykos exits, the ambiguities (last found in 727–8) give way to an explicit prediction of what awaits Lykos. The chorus follows with its prediction of the usurper's overthrow (734ff) and Lykos' cries are soon heard from within (750, 754). This pattern of events — entrance into the *skene*, 'words at the back', and choral prediction — is found several times in Euripides (see Chapter 4). The predicted murder does not always occur (cf. *Antiope*). Here the murder does take place, but a complete reversal follows. The scene between Amphitryon and Lykos is extremely brief in order not to disturb the mood of joy and celebration expressed in the two songs that frame it.[24] Lykos has to be killed, but he is treated as no more than another beast to be vanquished. The playwright focuses on Herakles' return and success.

After their immediate response to Lykos' death (755ff), the choristers begin the third stasimon proper (763–814). They continue in the ode the theme of divine justice that they have already pronounced (757ff). The ode sings not merely in joy and celebration, but in a belief in a theodicy as witnessed in Herakles' return and triumph.[25] The surprising entrance that follows not only ruptures the mood of joy but overturns the proclamations of divine justice.[26]

The ode complements the previous one: Herakles' homecoming is now complete with the punishment of Lykos. Together, and interrupted by only a very short scene, these two songs create the intense, almost palpable, mood of joy and faith. The third stasimon, however, ends with a trace of doubt in its final words, a rhetorical supposition (813–14):

If justice still is pleasing to the gods.

The hint of doubt,[27] though, seems no more than a whisper in the context of this and the preceding song and actions. But the whisper is answered by shouts of fear as the chorus cries out at the apparition above the house (815–17):

Ah! Ah!
Do we all now have the same fear,
Old men, since I see such a phantom above the house?

Iris and Lyssa have come to madden Herakles.[28] The joy of the ode has proved wrong: the gods are not just and Herakles' return is not triumphant after all. Not only is this appearance unexpected (perhaps it is the most surprising entrance in extant tragedy), it is unusual as well. The gods in Euripides, except for the special case of the 'mortal' Dionysos in *Bakch.*, appear only in the prologues, where they never interact with mortal characters, and at the end of the dramas. Secondly, this is the only instance of superhuman figures making a joint entrance. (The Dioskouroi, twins who always have only one speaking part, are different.) The unusual and sudden appearance of Iris and Lyssa completely reverses Herakles' fortune and the direction of the play.

After Iris returns to Olympos and Lyssa enters the house to wreak destruction on Herakles' family, the chorus predicts the death of the children (884–5). We experience this destruction in many stages: first Iris and Lyssa explain that they will cause the murders; the chorus in lyrics then predicts them; Amphitryon's[29] cries are heard from within, interspersed with choral laments; a messenger enters from the *skene* with a full description; and, finally, the *ekkyklema* is rolled out with the corpses and the subdued Herakles, while Amphitryon follows in on foot (see 1039–41). Herakles' murder of the children echoes his murder of Lykos, thus emphasising his painful change of fortune. The echo is especially pronounced by the similarities in the lyrics that attend the murders.[31] In both cases the chorus sings predominantly in dochmiacs, first alone (734–48/875–85), then in response to the cries heard from within (749–62/886–908). The second scene is more spectacular with the mention of both the earthquake (905)[32] and the appearance of Athene (906ff).

Before the *ekkyklema* is rolled out, the chorus responds to the messenger's eyewitness account with a brief astrophic song (1016–38), in which they proclaim that these murders surpass even those of the Danaids and Prokne. Comparing these murders to a mytho-historical event immediately before the corpses are seen, the chorus emphatically underscores the barbarity and terror of the deed. This final song is brief (*after* the *ekkyklema* and Amphitryon appear, i.e. at the start of the *next* scene, there is a lyric duet between the chorus and Amphitryon) because, having built up our expectations by revealing the murders in several stages, the poet now hastens to the 'ocular proof'.[33]

When the *skene* door opens at 1028 and the *ekkyklema* is rolled out, the chorus describes the corpses of Megara and the children, and Herakles tied to a pillar.[34] The lyric 'announcement' of this contraption (1028ff) both allows for it to be brought into position and adds to the importance of the moment, since announcements in lyrics are quite rare (see Chapter 4). This tableau reminds us of the drama's opening scene. The play began with the tableau of Amphitryon, Megara and the children at the altar. Now, not Megara and the children, but their corpses surround Herakles, who is tied to a pillar, which, like the altar, is a striking stage property. The supplication at Zeus' altar failed, and Herakles' rescue also failed: the now barren altar has not very far from it on stage this scene of divinely-wrought carnage about Herakles and the pillar.

The ensuing scene between Amphitryon and the chorus creates tension about the moment of Herakles' waking, as Amphitryon, fearful that his son may murder him as well, tries to quiet the chorus before they disturb the subdued hero.[35] When, however, it appears that Herakles is about to awaken, Amphitryon withdraws to one side of the stage (see 1081ff) and we wonder whether Herakles is still mad and will he attack his father.

As when he first entered at 523, Herakles, upon waking, has only limited vision of the stage, which in this case emphasises his confusion as he emerges from his sleep and attempts to get his bearings. *éa*, his first word (1089) marks his astonishment, and this is soon followed by confused questions when he does make contact with his surroundings, signalled by *idoú* at 1094. Just as Agave in *Bakch.* realises only in stages what she has done, so Herakles only gradually becomes aware of his murderous deeds. First he has only incomplete contact with the stage; then, when he makes fuller contact, he is shocked at what he sees; at last, in conversation with his father he learns of the murders. Ashamed of what he has done, Herakles decides on suicide, emphatically breaking off the stichomythia he had with his father in order to contemplate various methods (1146ff).

But the play does not end on this bleak note.[36] Theseus, who will rescue the rescuer, arrives and eventually persuades Herakles to live with him in Athens. Like Herakles and Iris and Lyssa, Theseus enters as a surprise. (He has been mentioned earlier in the play, 619–21, but we do not expect him at this point.) Thus the three *peripeteiai* of this play are all marked by surprise entrances. Herakles arrives after the possiblity of his arrival has been repeatedly denied; Iris and Lyssa appear completely out of the blue; and Theseus' entrance has had only the most minimal preparation. Herakles' first words when he sees Theseus approaching indicate that this entrance thwarts his suicide (1153–4):

> But interrupting my plans for suicide,
> Here comes Theseus, my kin and friend.

Theseus does not arrive after these two lines, but rather at 1163, about ten lines later. In the lines preceding this entrance Herakles expresses his shame at being seen by Theseus and his fear that his pollution will contaminate his friend. He veils his head (1159) in an attempt to hide his shame. Entering characters by convention do not hear the announcements that precede their arrivals,[38] and thus the poet here has the opportunity to display Herakles' reaction to Theseus' arrival — his deep fear and his shame — without Theseus' observing it.

Nowhere, I think, is the convention of 'partial vision' exploited more fully than in this play. Theseus upon his entrance does not notice the scattered corpses or Herakles. Like most entering characters, he initiates the dialogue, explaining to Amphitryon that he has arrived to bring aid to Herakles in return for the good deeds Herakles has done for him (1163–71). Then he notices the corpses, marking his recognition with the shout *éa*. Again we see the effectiveness of this convention. Taking Theseus by surprise in the middle of his speech, the scene of murder gains in its shock. While he enters and talks to Amphitryon, we are aware of the bodies and we await his recognition. When he does notice the bodies, our expectations are fulfilled. He does not notice Herakles until later (1189), and he does not actually see Herakles' face until the latter unveils himself at 1228. Like Herakles, Theseus makes contact and realises what has happened only in stages.

After a long debate, Theseus does persuade Herakles to continue living; and Herakles visually signals his acceptance of life when he decides to continue carrying his bow (1377ff). They will go to Athens and Amphitryon will remain and bury the children. Both stage actions and an unusual structure in the dialogue impress on us the impact of the separation of father and son. After Herakles accepts Theseus' invitation to be led to Athens, he desires to see the children and to embrace his father (1406ff). Theseus then reminds Herakles of his former valour, and finally Herakles bids farewell to his father and exits with Theseus, while Amphitryon exits into the *skene*.[39] Lines 1418 and 1420, spoken on departure, contain two changes of speaker, double *antilabé*, a striking feature that occurs only four other times in Euripides, and nowhere else in such proximity.[40] This unusual feature combines with the stage actions to add pathos to the departure. Amphitryon must go within and face the burial of the children, and Herakles is separated from the only member of his family he did not kill, the man whom he considers his 'real' father (cf. 1264–5).

Theseus leading Herakles off stage vividly recalls the exit before the second stasimon of Herakles, the protector of his family, leading them off to safety. The parallel between these two scenes is most striking: arriving in time to prevent their deaths at Lykos' hands, Herakles leads his family to apparent safety in the house, while Theseus comes on stage just in time to prevent Herakles from suicide. A distinct verbal echo strengthens the link between Herakles' two exits. When Herakles escorts the children into the house he refers to them as 'little boats ... in tow' (*epholkidas*, 631), while, as he exits with Theseus, he remarks (1423–4):[41]

> I, having destroyed my house with shameful deeds,
> All ruined, I will follow Theseus, a little boat in tow
> (*epholkides*).

We observed above that the first exit echoed the family's earlier entrance after the first stasimon and that the language of the family's announcement (442ff) is picked up in Herakles' exiting words (622ff). Thus language re-enforces the link among all three stage actions: the entrance of the family in funeral robes; their exit with Herakles; and Herakles' exit with Theseus.

There is a real progression in these three stage actions: in the first, the suppliants who had left the altar enter to apparent death; in the second, they exit, rescued from death, but the exit to safety is illusory; at the end of the drama, the final exit of Theseus with Herakles provides true safety. Herakles' concluding statement on friendship (1425–6) is no idle *sententia*. It echoes the ending of Amphitryon's opening *rhesis* (57–9) and points to what does endure in this play of sudden and violent turns of fortune. Herakles' protection of his family was short-lived. Even (especially?) the sons of gods are subject to the harsh blows of fortune and Hera. Theseus' friendship, however, proving itself in the test of difficulties, offers some solace and strength. The conquerer of so many beasts has himself been brought low, but with Theseus' friendship, he has at least survived.[42]

2. Troades

Tro., like several other Euripidean plays, commences with a divine prologue speaker: Poseidon enters,[43] explains why he has come, and relates the history and present circumstances of Troy. *Tro.* seems to begin as several other Euripidean plays do, but in fact it is extraordinary.

Bidding farewell to his dear city, Poseidon begins to exit (45–7):[44]

But, goodbye city that once was fortunate
And the polished walls. You would still be standing
If Pallas, Zeus' child, had not destroyed you.

Athene then appears,[45] delaying this exit; she wants to enlist his
aid in punishing the Greeks. This entrance surprises, and the surprise underlines the turnabout in Athene's design: a former patron
of the Greeks (alluded to in Poseidon's final lines, quoted above),
she now wants to punish them because of their offence to herself
and her temple (69). At the same time, Poseidon's farewell serves
as a bridge to her appearance ('talk of the devil'). The effect of
Athene's arrival is further highlighted by its abrupt delay of Poseidon's exit. The technique of delaying an exit by another arrival is
not uncommon in tragedy.[46] At *IA* 855, e.g., Achilleus has begun to
exit when the old man emerges from the *skene*, delaying his exit
with the crucial information of the intended sacrifice of Iphigeneia;
and the servant at *Hel.* 597 interrupts Menelaos' departure with
the startling news of the phantom Helen.[47] In these cases, and in
several others, the entrance that delays an exit is pivotal, as it
changes the course of events. The power of Athene's entrance here
has special point. By this forceful presentation of Athene's turning
against the Greeks, Euripides emphasises the punishment that
awaits them on their way home, and thus provides the backdrop of
the entire play. The continual suffering of the Trojans that we
witness on stage is only in seeming contrast to the victory of the
Greeks; they, too, the prologue scene informs us, will suffer. This
irony runs throughout the play, from Hekabe's opening laments to
the collapse of the city in the *exodos*.[48] The frequent references to
the Greeks' sailing home and the many nautical images (e.g. 102ff,
115ff, 137, 537ff, 686ff) remind us of this irony.[49] Athene's
surprise entrance also underlines the fickleness of the gods, a
theme of the drama: the gods, we repeatedly hear, have
abandoned once-great Troy and they can turn against Greek and
Trojan alike. (Poseidon himself draws attention to the inconstancy
of his niece — 59–60, 67–8.)

The divinities depart at 97 (or perhaps Athene exits a little
before — see 92), and Hekabe, alone on stage, prostrate in front of
the doors to the tents (see 37), begins in anapests her tale of woe.
Although she does not speak until this moment, she has been an
object of the spectators' concern since before the play began. The
actor playing Hekabe had to take up position on stage and then

later be 'discovered' by the audience, another example of a 'cancelled' first entrance. The situation in *Tro.*, however, is different from that of any other Euripidean play, because the discovery of the 'cancelled' entrance fully occurs only when Hekabe begins to speak at 98, not at the beginning of the drama. (*Or.* is dissimilar, because, although Orestes does not wake until 211, Elektra enters with him and delivers the opening monologue.) And only in *Tro.* is there another character on stage during the divine prologue scene. Perhaps we are reminded of Aischylos' famous silent characters, but in those cases a special emphasis is put on the silence or the breaking of it.[50] Here there is no mention of Hekabe's silence or her breaking it at 98, but she is the first person to catch the spectators' attention, Poseidon refers to her as prostrate and grieving (employing the deictic *ténd(e)* at 36) and she is visible to the audience throughout the divine prologue scene. Although she is not the explicit focus of attention, we cannot but see and wonder about the prostrate figure on stage. No one draws attention to Hekabe's silence for a very good reason — there is no one to do so. The divine prologue scene, even when another character is on stage during it, is detached in a sense from the action of the play. Poseidon does refer to her, but no dialogue can occur. The opening of this play is comparable to a 'split-screen' in film. On one 'side' we see the gods, while on the other we view the solitary and passive Hekabe.[51] Instead of bringing Hekabe on stage after this divine prologue scene (as he did in *Hek.*), Euripides with this staging from the very beginning presents her suffering and isolation.[52] The gulf between gods and mortals is also marked, as always in Euripidean prologue scenes, by the change in metre from the divinities to the mortal character who follows: Poseidon and Athene speak in iambic trimeter; Hekabe begins in anapests.

Hekabe is the dominant character of the drama: she is on stage from the very beginning to the closing moments, a sustained presence matched in extant tragedy only by Prometheus in *PB*.[53] Her pathos is given much attention, especially in this scene between the prologue and the entry of the chorus.[54] The chorus enters in two groups, at 153 and 176 respectively. The motivation for the first entrance, is their concern that Hekabe's cries, which they have heard from within (153–8) portend some new ill. The second group of Trojan women is called out (165–7), and they explain that they arrive to learn what awaits them (176ff). Perhaps Hekabe's final words before the first group enters help to prepare for these entrances (146−52):

> But like a mother
> I will lead (*exárxō*) for the winged birds
> A piercing song, very different
> From the ones which at one time,
> Leaning on Priam's sceptre
> Leading the chorus (*archechórou*) in Phrygian rhythms,
> I used to lead (*exêrchon*) in honour of the gods.[55]

The repetition (*exárxō, archechórou, exêrchon*) is emphatic; Hekabe, like a mother bird with her young, will lead the duet that follows. These women of the chorus share Hekabe's plight, and in this song the lamentations already heard are given new expression and development.

At the conclusion of this song the choristers wonder whither they will be taken, what city will hold them, now that Troy is gone. Immediately after the song, they announce in anapests the arrival of Talthybios. That there is any announcement at all directly after a strophic song is exceptional,[56] and this and the excited questions at the end of the announcement ('What news does he bring? What does he say?' 233) heighten the expectancy of the entrance. We have witnessed the pathetic situation of Hekabe and the other Trojan women and listened to the speculations about their futures, and now Talthybios arrives with the answers.

Kassandra, the first captive to be led away, makes a striking entrance at 308. Following his exchange with Hekabe (he in iambic trimeters, she in lyrics), explaining the lot of the various captives, Talthybios begins to fulfil his commands: he orders some of his men to bring out Kassandra so that he can lead her to Agamemnon (294−7). This is not the first time that Kassandra has been brought to our attention: her 'marriage' to Agamemnon is mentioned in the prologue scene (41−4); Hekabe expressly tells the chorus not to send her out of the tents (168ff); and Hekabe calls to her offstage to throw off her religious emblems (256−8) when she learns that Agamemnon will have her as his mistress. Perhaps Talthybios' men begin to execute his order. If so, they do not proceed very far when the herald cries out (298):

> Ah! What blaze of a torch shines within?

The shout drives our attention to the *skene* door, and we wonder along with Talthybios what is going on within: are the captives burning their quarters and themselves in despair (299–302)? Finally the herald bids someone to open the door. At that moment Hekabe announces that the captives are not killing themselves, but Kassandra is running out in a frenzied state, carrying a torch.[57] We are prepared for the entrance from the *skene,* but the manner is surprising. Not led forth by Talthybios' men, but of her own accord, Kassandra enters. She is in control not only of her entrance from the *skene,*[58] but also of the ensuing scene, and, in a sense, of her captor's fate. She suggests in this stage action what she articulates in the scene. When the former priestess rushes out in song and dance, carrying a torch, celebrating her impending marriage to Agamemnon in a wedding hymn, this seems grossly inappropriate to Hekabe. But it makes more sense as Kassandra explains, with gradual clarity, that the wedding will mean her victory over the enemy.[59] She continues to suggest her control as it is she who has the final words before departure (her *rhesis* at 424–61), words that spell out the fates in store for Odysseus and Agamemnon.[60] When they do depart at 461, Hekabe collapses in response to this latest grief, the loss of Kassandra (see 462ff). Prone as she was at the beginning of the drama,[61] she delivers a *rhesis* before the first stasimon. Again the audience focuses on Hekabe, who reveals more of her sad tale and intense suffering.

Inspired by Hekabe's closing *sententia* before the ode ('Of the prosperous/Consider no one fortunate, until he dies' (509–10)), the chorus describes the night Troy fell. The connection between an image in this ode and the following entrance was discussed in Chapter 4. In the epode describing the horrors of Troy's fall, the chorus depicts the suffering of children (557–9):

And dear infants
Were throwing their frightened arms
Around their mothers' robes.

The subsequent entrance vividly echoes this picture, as Andromache and her son enter in a wagon (568–71):

Hekabe, do you see Andromache here,
Carried in on the enemy's cart?

And her own Astyanax, Hektor's son,
Is at her heaving breast.

The suffering caused by the city's fall continues. (Later in this act Andromache, when she learns that her son is to be killed, asks the infant why he clings to her robes (750–1), another echo of the image in the ode.) Similarity in metre also links the end of the ode to this entrance. The epode is iambic, ending with syncopated iambic dimeters, and Andromache, after the announcement in anapests, begins with syncopated iambics as well.

This entrance of a 'moving tableau' (see Chapter 2) is impressive, and that it is a wagon not a chariot, which conveys the pair is significant. The Athenian spectators were not unfamiliar with chariots coming on stage with members of the royal household (e.g. Aisch. *Pers.* and *Ag.* and Eur. *El.*, probably produced not many years before). The simple wagon carrying Hektor's wife and son among other objects of spoil (573–4) deeply impresses the viewer, who makes the implicit comparison with the more usual chariot scene.

Talthybios' return (709) injects a new element into the action: not only is Andromache to be led away to serve Neoptolemos, but Astyanax, the herald reports, is to be killed in Troy. This entrance follows immediately after Hekabe has advised Andromache to yield to her new master, as distasteful as that might be, for one reason — so that she might rear Astyanax as the founder of a new Troy (697–705). The boy is held forth as the last hope for Troy; then Talthybios enters with the news to destroy this hope. The herald's ominous opening ('I wish I did not have to give this message', 711) and the gradual revelation of the news intensify the moment.

The conclusion of this scene visually presents the pathetic separation of mother and son. Towards the end of her attack on the Greeks, Andromache with bitter sarcasm invites the soldiers to kill and feast on her son (774–5). Perhaps Andromache, having handed over Astyanax as she made her invitation (or at the end of the speech), is carried off in the wagon. It is also possible that she does not leave the stage at this moment, and Talthybios[62] addresses Astyanax (782ff) while still in his mother's embrace. '*lambánet(e)*' ('Seize him', 786), then, is addressed to those who take the child from his mother directly. This is more economical in terms of stage actions — the infant is not passed from hand to hand

— and Talthybios' comments (786–9) are more forceful if he has at this moment separated mother and son, and not merely handed over the child to his men. The silence and passivity of Andromache while the herald calls the child to his death and the simultaneous exits in opposite directions (one to the ships, the other to the city) would be very affecting.[63] In either case, mother and son, both under someone else's power, are carried off stage while Hekabe remains. Again at the end of the scene we focus on Hekabe's sufferings in this 'tailpiece' to the act. She bewails her powerlessness to save Astyanax. Hekabe voices these laments in anapests. The act thus has a metrical frame: anapests announce the arrival and pronounce and lament the departure of Andromache and her child, while the body of the act, after the opening lyrics, is in spoken iambic trimeters.

After this most heinous act against Astyanax, the chorus in the second stasimon (799–859) declares that the gods have forsaken Troy. The city has been sacked twice, and even though Ganymede and Tithonos have had gods as lovers, the city has still been destroyed. The links between this song and Menelaos' following entrance (discussed in Chapter 4) are striking. His opening address to the sun's light (860) echoes the description of Eos in the ode's final stanza (847–50) and, following the narration of the two affairs with divinities that could not save Troy, Menelaos' arrival in search of Helen, whose affair with Paris led to the city's destruction, seems to confirm the validity of the song's closing line (858–9):

Troy's love charms over the gods are gone.

Love, the juxtaposition of song and entrance suggests, has not only not helped Troy, but destroyed it. Menelaos brings a new focus to the play. Hitherto we have watched the sufferings of Trojans; entrances have been either of victims or of Talthybios, who is orchestrating their sentences. Now Menelaos comes on stage, looking for his wife, who, we have frequently heard, is the cause of all this suffering. Euripides suggests a new direction for the drama by giving Menelaos' entering *rhesis* some qualities of a prologue.[64] We also note that by not recognising those on stage until Hekabe addresses him, he indicates his distance from and indifference to the plight of the Trojan women.[65]

After this opening *rhesis*, Menelaos sends some of his servants to bring Helen forth (880ff). While this order is being carried out,

Hekabe pleads with him (890ff) to kill his wife lest she seize him with desire. This warning, echoed at the close of this scene, articulates the issue of the scene: will Helen be punished? Although Helen is escorted from the *skene* by Menelaos' men, there is no anapestic announcement as for a 'moving tableau'. As we saw above,[66] such a treatment would be inappropriate for Helen, since it is employed elsewhere to arouse the audience's sympathy.

Helen's entrance (895) parallels those of Kassandra and Andromache earlier in the drama.[67] In all three of these cases the entering character is a female prisoner being led to her new, or in this case former, husband or lover. Maybe there is a subtle link between Kassandra's entrance and Helen's. The entrance of the priestess, we recall, was preceded by Talthybios' fear that the prisoners were burning down their quarters or themselves (299–302), and as Helen is about to enter, Hekabe warns Menelaos of her destructive force (892–3):

> She captures the eyes of men, she captures their cities,
> And *burns* their homes.

The first two entrances differ, of course, from the third. The first two women are Trojans, victims of the war, one of whom will be killed when she arrives in Greece, the other of whom will be a concubine for the son of her husband's murderer. The third is a Greek, the cause of the war's suffering, who is supposed to be killed at Troy, but who, we learn (876–9), will be brought back to Greece for her punishment. We, aware of the myth, realise that she will get off scot-free. The difference upon entrance also suggests the difference between the women. The Trojan women enter in lyric metres, Kassandra in a predominantly dochmiac song, and Andromache in lyric iambic rhythms, while Helen enters speaking calm iambic trimeters.

After the *agon* between Helen and Hekabe, where we see Helen at her sophistic best, pleading her poor case, Menelaos orders Helen to be led away (1047–8). Before he himself departs, Hekabe warns him not to let Helen set sail in the same ship lest desire for her prevent the punishment she deserves. This request echoes Hekabe's earlier plea (890ff), and thus her warnings begin and end the contest, reminding us by the fear that they express, that Helen, much as she might deserve it, will not suffer at all.

In the following, third stasimon (1060–1117), the chorus complains of the gods' abandonment of the city, its destruction and the women's present lot. The ending of this song is artfully juxtaposed to the next entrance: the chorus prays in the final stanza that Menelaos and Helen might meet their death on the deep (1100ff) (echoing the promise in the prologue of Greek disasters at sea), but directly following this wish is the entrance of the dead Astyanax, the antithesis of the prayed-for deaths. Talthybios, who enters with the corpse and speaks upon entering, is, contrary to the convention described in Chapter 2, not mentioned in the entrance announcement (1118–22). The break in the convention and the 'moving tableau', announced in anapests, both put the emphasis not on the Greeks' herald, but on the dead boy. Astyanax' exit to death and the return of his corpse surround the Helen scene. Effectively the death of the blameless child frames the sophistic and ultimately successful defence speech of the guilty Helen.

Talthybios exits at 1155 (having prepared for his return, 1153–5) to dig a grave for the boy, leaving Hekabe to make her long pathetic farewell to her grandson's corpse. After the lament and farewell of Hekabe and the chorus, the former bids servants to carry off the body for burial.[68] The chorus then sings a brief anapestic song (1251–9) in which they lament Andromache and her son. But the final blow has not yet been struck: the chorus now reports (1256ff) the sight of torches; the final destruction is at hand. These torches, as we observed in Chapter 2, do not appear on stage; the audience is asked to visualise the off-stage action when Talthybios, who enters at 1260, gives orders to those off-stage to put torches to the city (1260ff). Talthybios again is not announced, as attention is given to the incendiary destruction of the city and the thematically important torches. The destructive power of the torch has already been seen in the Kassandra scene, where we learn that her wedding torch will lead to the murder of Agamemnon. In the first play of the 415-group, *Alexandros*, the audience learned of Hekabe's dream that she would give birth to a blazing firebrand that would destroy the city and Helen clearly alludes to this at 919–22 of this play.[69] Hekabe's symbolic dream now comes to literal fulfilment with the incendiary destruction of Troy.

When the herald exits is uncertain. Either he departs at 1286 after his final commands to those who entered with him, or he remains on stage in silence and exits with Hekabe and the other Trojan women at the end of the play. I prefer the former staging.

The herald's final orders (1284–6) sound like exit lines and the last scene is better played out by the Trojan women alone, with the guards as unobtrusive mute characters.

Before considering this last scene, we should look at a famous passage from a preceding one, where Hekabe, in her lament over the dead Astyanax, takes solace in the fame of song (1242–5):

> If a god
> Had not upset us, turning things upside down,
> We would have disappeared and not be sung,
> Giving the themes for songs of future generations.

This passage, echoing Helen's remarks to Hektor in the *Iliad* (6. 357–8), must be heard in the context of the entire play. The royal house of Troy has been dissolved — one by one, Kassandra (who herself spoke of the fame brought by war, 394ff), Andromache, and Astyanax, the last hope for future Troy, are all led away to the ships or to be killed. Furthermore, in the contest with Helen, Hekabe won the argument, but lost her case. Now, as she sees her grandson's corpse and prepares it for burial, Hekabe reaches out for a new type of hope, fame in the song of later generations, traditional *kléos áphthiton*. The audience, watching *Tro.*, knows that the Trojan name has survived, but even this small solace is denied Hekabe. In response to Talthybios' orders to burn the city, Hekabe laments that Troy will be robbed even of its name (1277–8). And the chorus, in the final scene, twice echoes this despairing belief (1319, 1322–4).

In the play's finale, the chorus and Hekabe make their last laments, as they see and even feel (1325–6) the city's destruction. Visually this final scene recalls the opening of the drama: Hekabe returns to her original prone position, and the smouldering of Troy gives way to its fiery destruction. After the city's collapse, she rises (1327) and begins to exit, followed by the chorus. The drama, dominated by the continuous presence of Hekabe, the symbol of Trojan griefs, concludes when she makes her first, and last, exit. Although we, the audience, have been made aware in the prologue of the punishment that awaits the Greeks as they return home, and although Troy's fame will prove everlasting, Hekabe is unaware of the former and despairs of the latter. The irony of the Greek misfortunes and the knowledge of Troy's fame are enjoyed by the audience alone. No god descends to ameliorate the pain with a

vision of a different future, and the human friendship that concludes *Her.* is not seen here. It is the picture of Hekabe, a Trojan
of endless suffering, that leaves the final and indelible imprint on
our minds.

3. Ion

Hermes' prologue speech points to the role of divine providence in
this play.[70] Acting as Apollo's proxy, Hermes both narrates
Phoibos' concern for the infant Ion (28ff) and forecasts his future
handling of the affair: Ion will be given to Xouthos and revealed to
Kreousa in Athens (67ff). As the object of Apollo's concern is
about to enter, Hermes explains that he will get out of the way
(76–80):[71]

> But I will go into these laurel groves
> So I may learn well what awaits the boy.
> For I see Loxias' son coming forth,
> This one, so that he can make the temple's gateway bright
> With laurel branches.

We find this pattern several times in Euripides: a superhuman
figure alone on stage explains that he is exiting to avoid contact
with an approaching mortal character.[72] But Hermes' words
contain a difference from those of similar scenes: not merely is he
getting out of the way; he is going to learn how the child's fortunes
are accomplished. He assumes the role of the spectator, as it were,
waiting to learn the outcome of the drama.[73] Since events do not
turn out precisely as Hermes predicts, his spectator role is not
inappropriate. Even though the divine scheme does not go exactly
as planned, the role of the divine is seen in the interruption of the
poisoning of Ion (see 1563ff) and in the entrances of the priestess
and Athene later in the drama. As in *Tro.*, the divine prologue
creates an ironic backdrop for the play: this divine plan is
unknown to Kreousa until the play's end and against it we witness
her harsh and at times passionate attacks on Apollo. And yet even
at the close of the drama with its 'happy' ending, the audience
must weigh this divine plan against the earlier actions of Apollo,
the many acts and near-acts of violence in the play caused by those
actions, and the deeply felt and movingly expressed suffering of
Kreousa.

Immediately before Ion enters, Hermes, in his final words, gives the boy his name (80–1):

And with the name he is about to receive
I first of the gods name him — Ion.

Later in the play (661ff) we learn that the name stems from Xouthos meeting Ion first when Xouthos emerged from Apollo's temple. This scene prefigures the later one: Ion is named at his entrance as later he will be 'found' and named at Xouthos. Verbal echoes, we have seen, also link Hermes' prologue to Ion's entrance. As described in Chapter 4, Hermes' use of 'bright' (*lamprá*, 79) is echoed in the three-fold repetition of words from that root in Ion's opening lines (82, 83, 87). When Ion enters with attendants (see 94ff) he speaks in anapests. Although the gods are exceptionally concerned with Ion's welfare, a gulf still separates gods and men: Hermes speaks in iambic trimeter, Ion in anapestic dimeter.

As is not infrequently the case (*Tro.* provides a clear example) the slot between the prologue speech(es) and the chorus' entry often focuses on the emotions of one character. Here we observe the joyful and carefree life of Apollo's servant. Ion's purity and naïveté will be threatened in the course of the drama, and this scene provides a contrasting picture for the subsequent events. Yet even here Ion's violence is suggested when he draws his bow against the birds (158ff).[74] Later he will draw his bow against Xouthos (524) and threaten to kill Kreousa.

The chorus enters (184) after Ion's monody without an announcement. Since only Ion is on stage, no announcement is expected, but it is striking that no contact is made between Ion and the chorus until the latter addresses him at 219.[75] The lack of contact is atypical but explicable. Euripides' elaborate description of the Delphic temple is unique in extant tragedy;[76] it is, among other things, a *tour de force*. The entering chorus is so caught up in the splendour of the sight that they make no contact with the temple's custodian, who presumably continues with his tasks. (Again we have a type of 'split-screen': Ion at his tasks and the 'tourists' enjoying the sights.) The excitement and joy of this scene continue until Kreousa enters.

Kreousa, the chorus' mistress, arrives at the end of the *parodos*. Most unusually,[77] she is announced in the lyrics (237), as the chorus explains to Ion that Kreousa herself can answer his questions. Her entrance differs from that of the chorus. They did not address Ion at once because they were overwhelmed by the temple's decorations; Kreousa, on the other hand, reminded by the temple (249ff) of Apollo's treachery, is too caught up in her grief (241ff) to do so.[78] Euripides, by this arrangement, not only displays Kreousa's grief, but is also able to reveal Ion's sensitivity and compassion as he begins the dialogue. Upon first seeing Kreousa, he exclaims at her nobility (237–40), then he recognises that she is crying, and finally (244–6) he asks her questions to which she replies.

In their conversation, carried on mainly in a long and splendid stichomythia (264–368), Ion and Kreousa both reveal their sympathies for one another and marvel at the similarities of their situations (see, e.g., 320, 359–60). In fact, Kreousa — even with her false tale of her 'friend' — and Ion seem on the verge of a true recognition. The stichomythia (and the premature recognition) is broken off when Ion, defending his patron god, explains that the god will not answer the hostile questions that Kreousa would pose to him. Kreousa replies with an attack on Apollo for his offences against her 'friend', an attack which she must break off when she see Xouthos approaching (392ff).

Xouthos receives a long entrance announcement (392–400), during which Kreousa, as soon as she sees him coming, asks Ion to keep what she has revealed secret from her husband. The secrets between husband and wife will, of course, prove almost fatal to both Ion and Kreousa in the course of the play. At the moment of Xouthos' first entrance, these secrets are stressed. Kreousa's request for secrecy extends beyond the requirements of the plot, as it reveals both the natural rapport between Ion and herself and the distance she maintains from her husband. Xouthos' entrance comes relatively late in the act: it is more than three-quarters finished.[79] After the long scene between Kreousa and Ion, in which they show a mutual sympathy for each other, Xouthos appears like an outsider, which in many ways, the play reminds us, he is.[80] Xouthos, when he first arrives, notices Kreousa's disturbed state (402–03), but he shows less concern than did Ion, and Kreousa does not want to reveal her secrets and feelings to him. The information that Xouthos brings, that Trophonios has predicted that neither he nor Kreousa will leave childless, contrasts with Kreousa's statement before she announces his arrival that Apollo will not answer her 'friend's' questions (387–9). Xouthos, who in the next scene will joyously embrace Ion as his son, takes no notice of the young man and neither refers to nor addresses him at any point in the scene. Xouthos' question 'Who is the interpreter for the god?' (413) is not directed to Ion and, as soon as he receives a reply from the temple's servant, he exits. Although Xouthos perhaps has no special reason to converse with this young man, Euripides allows no contact between these two in order to contrast their encounter with the just-observed Kreousa-Ion scene and to emphasise the reversal in the next act.

After Xouthos exits into the *skene* (424), Kreousa, after another, brief attack on Apollo, departs down one of the *parodoi* (428). She does not address these lines to Ion, but they are not an aside — he hears them.[81] Ion exits soon after Kreousa, at 451. As we saw above in the discussion of *Her.*, successive exits of three characters are extremely rare. Euripides here achieves two important effects with this pattern. First, it highlights Ion's 'tailpiece' at the conclusion of the act (429–51). The young man's staunch belief in his patron deity has been shaken, and this is the first opportunity to have him express his doubts about Apollo and the other gods. Secondly, the successive exits convey the separateness of the three persons involved. Xouthos and Kreousa are both looking for a son, but their mutual success in finding him involves the deception of Xouthos, and their devious machinations (as well as the god's) prevent any union of the three. This is the only scene in which all three characters appear together; they are on stage together for a scant twenty-four lines and then they exit severally — each perhaps in a different direction.[82]

In the following triadic ode (452–509) the chorus sings of childbirth and in the first stanza invokes Athene and Artemis to bring forth a child for the race of Erechtheus, Kreousa's family, and at the end of the song refers to the tale of the girl exposing the child, Kreousa's child. The subsequent scene, where we witness the false recognition of Xouthos and Ion, contrasts sharply with the song. Not Kreousa, but Xouthos, it seems, has received a child. The entries after the ode of Ion and Xouthos are virtually simultaneous, perhaps suggesting the fortuitousness involved.[83] Ion arrives on stage first, inquiring whether Xouthos has returned from the temple; the chorus replies negatively and then announces that he has just emerged from the temple (515–16):

But I hear a noise from these doors, like someone leaving,
And now one can see my master coming out (*exiónta*).

éxeimi is almost never used in entrance announcements; at most
there is one other instance in Euripides.[84] After Hermes has
named the boy at 80–1 and directly before the false recognition
takes place, this might be a mild paronomasia for the audience.
Xouthos, following Apollo's oracle (explained at 535–6), takes the
first person he encounters when he leaves the temple as his son
and so addresses him in his opening words (517). Xouthos, indifferent to the boy in the previous scene, is eager to embrace him.
Shocked, Ion rebuffs the man and even threatens him with his bow
(524). The recognition is finally achieved, but not without Ion's
expression of many doubts and fears about leaving for Athens.
'Father' and 'son' then begin to exit to celebrate the 'birthday'.
Near the end of this scene, Xouthos gives Apollo's servant the
name Ion and explains the name (note *exiónti*, 662); thus this
wordplay virtually frames the act (515–16, 661–3). Ion closes the
act with the wish that his mother might be an Athenian so that he
might enjoy the free speech of an Athenian. His mother enters at
the beginning of the next act and therein plots his murder; when
we next see Ion, he is pursuing his mother in order to stone her.

Xouthos and Ion depart at 675 (the former disappears entirely
from the play). The choristers are upset at the turn of events. In
their song (676–724), they sympathise with Kreousa, doubt the
oracle's validity, and condemn the actions of Xouthos. The epode,
although textually corrupt, clearly ends with a prayer for the boy's
death and, in the final words, an emphatic reference to Erechtheus, from whom stems the proper succession to Athenian rule.[85]
Kreousa, as the name Erechtheus still rings in our ears, enters with
an old household servant, whom she addresses in her opening
words (725–6): 'Old man, tutor of Erechtheus, my late father'.
The verbal link is clear; and in this scene the Erechtheidai will take
action against the apparent usurper.

Kreousa's and the old servant's entrance is drawn out, emphasising the age and sluggishness of movement of the latter.[86] This
long entrance description increases the tension: although Xouthos
has threatened the chorus with death if they reveal his discovery to
Kreousa (666–7), in the subsequent lyric they expressed their evil
wishes against the ursurper. Will they tell Kreousa what they have
been commanded not to, but what they have suggested they would

in the lyric (695ff)? This is what the audience wonders when Kreousa and the family retainer enter, and the suspense is heightened when the chorus cannot decide whether to tell Kreousa or not (752ff).[87] Kreousa at last learns of Xouthos' child and deceit,[88] and the servant and she plot revenge by murdering Ion, a plot that is interrupted by Kreousa's impassioned monody (859–922). The two exit separately, Kreousa somewhat before (see 1039–40) and the servant at 1047, after a few closing remarks. His appeal to his aged foot to be young again (1041–2) might suggest that he exits at a quicker pace than when he entered. His exit then responds to his entrance: he is rejuvenated in the service of his mistress.[89]

A messenger comes on stage (1106) after the next stasimon (1048–1105) looking for Kreousa, and he reports the foiled attempted murder. In the stasimon the chorus had prayed for and urged on Ion's murder and concluded with a harsh condemnation of Xouthos. This prayer is answered negatively with the messenger's report. (We should note the juxtaposition of the song's end and the messenger's opening line: the chorus' final words condemned Xouthos for 'obtaining a bastard son' (1105) and the messenger begins by enquiring as to the whereabouts of *Erechtheus'* daughter (1106–7).) Just as the second messenger in *IT* reports the failed escape of Iphigeneia and comrades, this speech narrates the failed assassination attempt. Typically a messenger's speech reports a completed action, the results of which we see shortly thereafter. Here the report relates a failed action and serves as a foil to the exciting scene that follows: Ion will threaten to murder the one who tried to murder him, his mother. The messenger's purpose in coming on stage also is unsuccessful. He is looking for Kreousa but, not finding her, he exits to continue his search.

The pace of the drama now increases greatly. Only a brief astrophic song (1229–43) and a few lines of anapests (1244–9) intervene before the next entrance. There is no escape, the chorus proclaims. As we approach the climax of the drama, the poet gives little time to lyric reflection. The successive and rapid entrances of Kreousa and Ion and the use of trochaic tetrameters (1250–60) quicken the action. Kreousa enters at 1250 and Ion and allies at 1261, both entries on the run.[90] Kreousa's entrance, as we saw above in Chapters 2 and 3, is not announced in the preceding anapests, rather these anapests serve as a 'talk of the devil' link to her appearance. The chorus has asked what more Kreousa can suffer (1246–7) and wonders if they are not being punished justly

(1247–9). Kreousa then rushes on stage, crying that she is being pursued and threatened with death. The answer to the chorus' question now begins to be played out on stage.

Kreousa, although initially skeptical about the altar's value for her (1255ff), accepts the choral advice of supplication at the altar (repeated as an imperative at 1258) after she sees the approaching men (1257ff), and begins to head towards it. Her movement towards the altar and the subsequent motion of Ion's men to capture her (following Ion's command at 1266ff) are stylised, slow actions, the same kind that we observed at *Her.* 514ff.[91] As the men approach Kreousa, who is proceeding towards the altar, Ion continues his attack on her. By 1279 she has taken up her position at the altar, and Ion's words at 1279ff acknowledge this and implicitly refer to the non-performance of the order to seize her. After the rapid successive entrances at 1250 and 1261, Euripides slows down the tempo to stress the action of this moment:[92] Kreousa, who has been at odds with Apollo throughout the play, now puts her life in his hands by supplicating his altar (see 1283),[93] while Ion, her son, denounces her and threatens her with death.

Ion is stymied by this action: he is caught in the dilemma of punishing the woman who tried to murder him or reverencing the altar of his patron Apollo, where she has taken refuge. As much as he might condemn and argue with Kreousa, he cannot bring himself to violate the right of this suppliant. He ends the stichomythia with Kreousa (1312) in order to ponder the injustice of the altar offering protection to the unjust. The drama has reached an impasse: Kreousa has the altar's protection and Ion is at a loss about what to do. At this juncture we might expect a *deus ex machina* to break the deadlock. Apollo could appear to effect the recognition and to mend a few fences. If we anticipate this, we are frustrated in our expectations. The divine plan does take control, but it is the temple's priestess,[94] Apollo's proxy, not the god himself, who suddenly, without preparation[95] or announcement, emerges from the *skene* with Ion's birth tokens. (Her command to Ion as she enters, '*episches*' (1320), is, we have seen, typical for preventing violent actions.) She explains (1341ff) that she both kept these tokens in silence and now brings them forth at Apollo's bidding. She instructs Ion to look for his mother and bids him farewell, exiting at 1368. After her departure, Ion is still confused and wonders what he should do with the tokens. Perhaps they will show that a slave was his mother, he fears (1382ff). He concludes

(1387ff), however, that the god wants him to search for his mother
and he thus begins to examine the tokens. Kreousa recognises
these tokens as the ones she left with her exposed child, and leaves
the altar to claim her son. Although divine power precipitated the
prophetess' appearance, a human act of faith — Kreousa risking
her life in leaving the altar — achieves the recognition. Kreousa has
not said a word since 1311. While Ion speculates about the injustice of the altar's protection and receives the tokens from the priestess and wonders about what to do with them, Kreousa is silent.
We know that they are mother and son, and once the prophetess
produces the birth tokens we expectantly await the recognition.
But Euripides draws out the scene, as Kreousa, who can identify
the tokens, remains at the altar without a word. When she does
claim the tokens and her son, the breaking of this silence underscores the importance of the action.[96]

We thus witness the play's second, and true, recognition, a
recognition that echoes in both actions and language the false
recognition of Xouthos and Ion.[97] In each scene the parent claims
the boy as his/her son (note the greeting *ô téknon* at both 517 and
1399) and attempts to establish this claim with an embrace
(Xouthos tries to embrace the boy, 523ff, Kreousa the tokens,
1404ff). Ion thinks they are mad (520, 1402) and rebuffs them,
threatening Xouthos with his bow (524ff) and Kreousa with
seizure (and, as this implies, death, 1402ff), but each parent is willing to risk his life (527, 1401). Interrogated by Ion, each one is
finally accepted by the convinced boy, and the acceptance is
marked by an embrace (560ff, 1437ff). Striking verbal correspon-
dences also help to connect these two scenes. When Xouthos goes
to embrace Ion at 523, he explains:

> I will hold you. I am not confiscating property, but claiming my
> own.

Both the very rare (in tragedy) word *rhusiázō* ('confiscate
another's property') and *heuriskō* ('find, claim') are found also in
the second recognition when Kreousa claims Ion with an embrace
of the tokens (1406–7):

> Ion: Isn't this dreadful? I am confiscated (*rhusiázomai*) by
>   stealth.
> Kr.: No, but you are found (*heuriskēi*) kin to your kin.

In this play of multiple ironies and reversals, this second and true recognition mirrors and corrects the first. The scenes differ in two important respects. The recognition of Kreousa and Ion is followed, as is typical after such recognitions in tragedy, by a lyric duet of celebration (1439ff). No such lyric rejoicing followed the false recognition. Secondly, the tone distinguishes the two recognitions. The audience can enjoy the somewhat lighthearted encounter between Xouthos and Ion (including the former's explanation of his youthful indiscretions). Xouthos' life is threatened only by his advances towards Ion,[98] while Kreousa's life is in real jeopardy because of her attempted murder. The recognition between Kreousa and Ion is filled with tension. We have heard again and again about her suffering at the hands of Apollo; she is, we know, the true parent of this young man; and now she most fully risks her life to claim her child. The lyric duet that follows this second recognition not only helps to distinguish it from the first but is an appropriate and welcome relief after this scene.

Ion, however, is not quite satisfied with Kreousa's story and decides to question Phoibos himself on these matters (as he had told Kreousa was impossible, 369ff). He heads towards the *skene* door in search of Apollo, and the seasoned theatre-goer might expect Apollo *ex machina*, but again the spectator is thwarted in his expectations. Ion announces the advent of the divinity (1549–52), and there is even a hint that the appearance is that of Apollo, since Ion describes the divine presence as follows (1549–50):

Ah! What god shows forth above this temple
A face like the sun?

antélion ('like the sun') might suggest Apollo, since he has been subtly associated with it throughout the play.[99] But Athene,[100] not Apollo, appears. Ion begins to exit into the *skene* to question Apollo, but a different god from a different place, Athene *ex machina*, arrives. For the third time in this play (Hermes' and the priestess' appearances are the first two) not Apollo, but a proxy for him, appears.

Again the gods have intervened. Athene, like Hermes, is acting on Apollo's behalf, and these two divine appearances thus neatly frame the action of the play. After explaining Apollo's designs and the greatness of Ion's future progeny, Athene bids Ion and

Kreousa to proceed to Athens, and thither they exit. The goddess departs and the choristers follow their mistress out after their coda (1619–22). Only twice in this play do two persons exit together; all other exits are of one person or of the chorus. Once Xouthos and Ion depart as 'father and son' after the false recognition, and now Kreousa and Ion, finally and firmly reunited as mother and son, exit towards Athens. This exit, like the second recognition, reverses the previous one. Ion has assured Athene that his doubts are gone (1606ff) and Kreousa has forgiven Apollo (1609ff). If the audience has not forgotten the previous griefs and violence, the characters, at least, seem satisfied. Kreousa has her son, Ion his mother and the rule of Athens. The gods, and mortals, have found a way.

Notes

1. See Taplin, 134–6, and the bibliography cited there.
2. Of course not only in 'suppliant' plays does the chorus arrive in such sympathy with a character on stage or about to come on stage; cf., e.g., *Alk.*, *Hipp.*, *Or.*
3. That they do nothing to prevent Herakles' murder of the children does not, *pace* Bond (ed.), 91, suggest their helplessness. The audience cannot expect any mortal to thwart that divinely-caused action.
4. See Taplin, 283–4.
5. On the structure of this speech, see Bond (ed.), 102.
6. On the parallels between these two scenes, see above, Chapter 4.
7. Wilamowitz (ed.), vol. 3, 38, correctly observes that Lykos' speech functions as a foil for Amphitryon's reply (170–235), and, as Bond (ed.), 101–2, notes, no other *agon* has such a disparity in the length of speeches. But the initial impression Lykos gives is, as I suggest, one of dominance, and, although he loses the verbal argument, he defeats the suppliants in actions.
8. That *all* of them are going to put on these clothes seems most probable from Lykos' remarks now (333ff) and later (702–3) and Megara's after Herakles return (549). See Bond (ed.), 204.
9. We cannot be certain that Megara and the children exit prior to and not with Amphitryon, but Megara's command that the children accompany her into the house strongly suggests a departure at 338. Wilamowitz, Parmentier-Grégoire, and Bond all concur; Bodensteiner does not.
10. On suppliants in general, see J. Gould, 'Hiketeia', *JHS* 93 (1973), 74–103; on Euripidean altar scenes, see the bibliography cited by Gould, 89 n. 76. A.P. Burnett in her interpretation of the play (*Catastrophe Survived: Euripides' Plays of Mixed Reversal* (Oxford 1971, 157–82) makes too much of this act of leaving the altar. For a good response to her interpretation of the play and a proper appreciation of this important book, see B. Knox (rev.), *CP* 67 (1972), 270–9 = *Word and Action: Essays on the Ancient Theater* (Baltimore and London 1979), 329–42.

11. See A.M. Dale, *Collected Papers* (Cambridge 1969), 180–4, on such 'challenging-nouthetetic' prayers.

12. For the motif of dual parentage and its importance in the play, see J. Gregory, 'Euripides' *Heracles*', *YCS* 25 (1977), 259–75.

13. Bond (ed.), 152, comments that *eite . . . eite* (353ff) is formulaic in such a context. But its formulaic nature does not lessen the echo of Amphitryon's challenge or, as Bond himself observes, its 'touch of rationalist speculation'.

14. The earliest references to the lion skin's invincibility are Pindar, *Isth.* 6, 47–8, and Bakchylides 13, 53ff. For more on the invincibility of the skin, see A. Henrichs, ('Zur *Meropis*: Herakles' Löwenfell und Athenas zweite Haut', *ZPE* 27 (1977), 69–75.

15. For the textual problem of 446, see Bond (ed.), *ad loc.* I translate the conjecture *hupóseira.* Whichever of the proposed remedies is adopted, the echoes of these lines later in the play are clear.

16. See Wilamowitz (ed.), vol. 3, 84–6.

17. *teleután* possesses, of course, an ambiguity, but the chorus emphasises only one side of the ambiguity.

18. See the discussion of this scene in Chapter 3.

19. They do not do so at once, as the text makes clear. Bain, *Actors and Audience: A Study of Asides and Related Conventions in Greek Drama* (Oxford 1977), 63, comments, 'Actions on one half of the stage reaches a standstill so that all attention may be fixed upon Hercules' soliloquy. On 'slow' or 'frozen' movements on the tragic stage, see Mastronarde, 2–3, 110–12.

20. See H. Parry, 'The Second Stasimon of Euripides' *Heracles* (637–700)', *AJP* 86 (1965), 363–74.

21. *aretâi* (697) is Nauck's conjecture, accepted by, among others, Murray, Parmentier-Grégoire, and Diggle.

22. H. Parry. *The Lyric Poems of Greek Tragedy* (Toronto and Sarasota 1978), 160.

23. Lykos addresses Amphitryon in his opening line (adopting Heath's conjecture *peráis*).

24. As Wilamowitz (ed.), vol. 3, 159–60, comments, this scene is only a bridge between the two songs.

25. A. Lesky, *Greek Tragic Poetry*, (trans.) M. Dillon (New Haven 1983) 277, notes the symmetry of the ode: the two strophes cry out for celebration and the two antistophes announce the justice of the gods.

26. Bond (ed.), 263–4, points to the 'intellectual flavor' of the ode, which he finds lacking in the *parà prosdokian* odes of Sophokles.

27. Parry, above, n. 22,; 161–2, comments on what he feels are some ambiguities in the earlier section of the lyric and the ode proper (e.g. 736, 738, 740, 765, 766, 777), ambiguities which suggest that Herakles, like Lykos, is subject to a change of fortune. The ambiguities of these words might appear retrospectively, and the audience is certainly forced to realise that the theodicy expounded in this ode (and elsewhere) operates, if it operates at all, differently from the way they had first supposed. But it seems to me that at this point the emphasis falls strongly on the joy and celebration so that the subsequent reversal of Herakles' fortunes is that much more surprising and shocking.

28. On the problems of staging this scene, esp. that of the 'chariot', see Bond (ed.), 280, 299–300, and Hourmouziades, 162.

29. That the cries from within are meant to be Amphitryon's, see Wilamowitz, (ed.), *ad loc.*

30. On the use of the *ekkyklema* for this scene, see Hourmouziades, 98ff.

31. See Bond (ed.), 295, on these similarities.

32. Although it is possible, there is no reason to assume that this earthquake

was staged or accompanied by noise offstage; see, e.g., Dodds (ed.), *Bakch.*, 148–9, and A.M. Dale, above n. 11, 124–5.

33. We observed above, Chapter 4 n. 50, that the final choral songs of a tragedy tend to be briefer than the earlier ones.

34. On this scene and a comparison between it and the similar one in Soph. *Aias*, see H. Ortkemper, *Szenische Techniken des Euripides: Untersuchungen zur Gebärdensprache im antiken Theater* (Diss. Berlin 1969), 93ff.

35. We should compare *Or.*, 132–210. On the verbal similarities between the two scenes, see Bond (ed.), 332–3.

36. Taplin, 180–4, includes this play among those containing a 'false ending'.

37. See Burnett, above n. 10, 173ff, on the final section of this play.

38. For the rare exceptions to this convention, see Taplin, 72–3.

39. See Hourmouziades, 104.

40. On double *antilabē* see W. Köhler, *Die Versbrechung bei den griechischen Tragikern* (Diss. Giessen, Darmstadt 1913), 42–3. He also observes (13–17) that *antilabē* is common in scenes of parting. We might also observe that 1418 contains not only two changes of speaker, but three different speakers; this is without parallel in Euripides.

41. The first to note this echo was, I think, Wilamowitz (ed.), vol. 3, 280. S. Barlow, *The Imagery of Euripides* (London 1971), 107–8, mentions the link among all three actions, as I do below.

42. I do not mean to suggest, as does H. Chalk, '*Aretē* and *bia* in Euripides' *Herakles*', *JHS* 82 (1962), 7–18, that Herakles replaces the old *aretē* with the new one of friendship; see e.g. A.W.H. Adkins' response to Chalk, 'Basic Greek Values in Euripides' *Hecuba* and *Hercules Furens*'. n.s. 16 (1966), 209–19.

43. See Hourmouziades, 160–2, for a discussion of possible stagings of this and Athene's entrance.

44. Poseidon, predominantly pro-Greek in Homer (but see *Il.* 20, 290ff where he rescues Aineias) is pro-Trojan here (and at *IT* 1414–15); on Poseidon's sympathies in this play (with the Trojans or merely the walls he built with Apollo) see the exchange between J. Fontenrose and J.R. Wilson in *Agon* 1, 2 (1967, 1968), 135–41, 66–71.

45. See the discussion of this entrance above, Chapter 2.

46. For delayed exits caused by another's entrance, see Taplin, esp. 162–3, 299–300.

47. These entrances were discussed above in Chapters 2 and 3 respectively.

48. A full treatment of this ironic function of the prologue is E. O'Neill, Jr., 'The Prologue of the *Troades* of Euripides', *TAPA* 72 (1941), 288–320.

49. On the nautical imagery in this play, see S. Barlow, above n. 41, 29–30, 51–2, 118.

50. The character Euripides in Aristophanes' *Frogs* (911ff; and see the scholia *ad loc.*) criticised this Aischylean practice. A stimulating treatment of this practice is O. Taplin, 'Aeschylean Silences and Silences in Aeschylus', *HSCP* 76 (1972), 57–97. He refers to the opening of *Tro.* at 96 n. 118 only to suggest the possibility of the influence of Aisch. *Niobe*; he concludes that the connection between the two plays is only remote.

51. W. Steidle, *Studien zum antiken Drama* (Munich 1968), 50–2, remarks on the passivity of Hekabe throughout the play, in part emphasised by her frequent prostrate position. See also J. de Romilly, *L'Evolution du pathétique d'Eschyle à Euripide* (Paris 1961), 80–1.

52. The prologue emphasises that Troy itself is deserted (note *erēma*, 15; *erēmia*, 26; *erēmiai*, 97), a description of the backdrop which parallels Hekabe's own isolation.

53. On the similarities between the early sections of these two plays, see H.

Schmidt, 'Die Struktur des Eingangs' in W. Jens (ed.), *Die Bauformen der griechischen Tragödie* (Munich 1971), 26–7.

54. See Taplin, 246–7, for the pathos and isolation frequently depicted in the slot between the prologue proper and the chorus' entry that is characteristic of Euripides.

55. Diggle daggers 147–8; I translate Parmentier's text. For a discussion of the textual problems, see Lee (ed.), *ad loc.*, whose interpretations of the text I generally follow.

56. See our earlier treatment of this entrance and its announcement in Chapter 2.

57. *thoázei* (307) suggests her frenzied state; see *LSJ thoázō* (A) 2 and Lee (ed.), *ad loc.* On the importance Kassandra places on the torch, see Barlow, above n. 41, 53.

58. Cf. the control of the *skene* door in Aisch. *Ag.* (where it has greater significance), and Taplin's discussion of it, 306ff.

59. The pattern of lyrics followed by spoken iambics leading from confusion to greater clarity is found elsewhere in Euripides (cf., e.g., *Hipp.* 198ff) and is seen most dramatically in the Kassandra scene in Aisch. *Ag.*

60. Having the final words upon exiting often suggests control of the situation. Perhaps the best example of this in Greek tragedy is in Soph. *OT*, where Oidipous stands dumb while he listens to Teiresias, another prophet, forecast in riddles the soon-to-occur disastrous self-revelation (447–62); both men then exit right after these riddling lines. See Taplin, *Greek Tragedy in Action* (Berkeley and Los Angeles 1978), 43–4.

61. Hekabe assumes another prone position at the end of this act (see 505ff). At what point she rises again is uncertain — perhaps as Andromache is announced. Hekabe's risings and fallings in this play are not always clearly indicated in the text. Steidle, above n. 51, basically following Wilamowitz (trans.), makes several suggestions for these stage actions. All are possible, some probable, but only of a few can we be certain.

62. Taplin, 91 n. 2, argues that we should retain the mss. reading *humetéras* (788) and give 782–9 to Andromache. Although I think that Andromache does not exit until 789, I am unconvinced that these final lines are hers. In addition to the dramatic reasons given above, we should also note that it would be unusual for Andromache to resume, after a brief choral buffer, this time in a different metre.

63. It is, of course, also possible that Andromache hands over the child at 775 (or 779) and remains silent during Talthybios' anapests. Possible, but, I think, less effective.

64. On the prologue qualities of this speech, see F. Leo, *Der Monolog im Drama: Ein Beitrag zur griechisch-römischen Poetik* Abh. Ges. Wiss. Göttingen phil-hist. Kl. N.F. 10.5 (Berlin 1908), 30, and W. Schadewaldt, *Monolog und Selbstgespräch: Untersuchungen zur Formgeschichte der griechischen Tragödie*, Neue Philologische Untersuchungen 2 (Berlin 1926), 101 n. 1 and 241.

65. Mastronarde, 24–6, notes that Menelaos has no reason to address Hekabe or the chorus. True, but this does not lessen the effect of his ignoring them until Hekabe speaks.

66. Chapter 2 n. 51. Such an entrance announcement would be inappropriate, and any announcement is unnecessary, since, as already noted in the earlier discussion, Helen has been sent for; hers is an 'Ersatz' announcement.

67. Others have noted the parallels among these three scenes; see, e.g., W. Friedrich, *Euripides und Diphilos*, Zetemata 5 (Munich 1953), 73–5, and Steidle, above n. 51, 52–4.

68. These servants probably enter from the *skene* at 1207 and exit with the corpse later (see 1246ff); see Lee (ed.), 265–6.

69. See *Alexandros* fr. 1 Snell, and on the thematic image of the torch, R. Scodel, *The Trojan Trilogy of Euripides*, Hypomnemata 60 (Göttingen 1980), 76–8.

70. Among recent critics who have discussed the 'divine plan' at work in *Ion*, see A.P. Burnett, 'Human Resistance and Divine Persuasion in Euripides' *Ion*', *CP* 57 (1962) 89–103, and C. Wolff, 'The Design and Myth in Euripides' *Ion*', *HSCP* 69 (1965), 169–94. Of course, as the play demonstrates, not everything goes according to this plan. See R. Hamilton, 'Prologue Prophecy and Plot in Four Plays of Euripides', *AJP* 99 (1978), 279–83, on the differences between the divine prophecy and its fulfilment.

71. Whither Hermes exits is not clear. If he exits into the *skene*, he can avoid Ion, who is entering from it (*ekbainonta*, 78) only if there is more than one *skene* door (which seems to me probable in the last quarter of the fifth century). If he exits down one of the *parodoi*, how are 'these laurel groves' represented? As is evident from the discussion of divine prologues in Chapter 2, I do not think the prologue was delivered from the roof. With some reservations I opt for an exit into a side door of the *skene*, which would in part represent these groves. See Wilamowitz (ed.), 23 and *ad loc.*, and Hourmouziades, 157ff.

72. See our discussion above in Chapter 2.

73. The actor, of course, does not remain on stage; see n. 71 above.

74. See C. Whitman, *Euripides and the Full Circle of Myth* (Cambridge, Mass. 1974), 69–103, for a discussion of violence and purity, among other themes, in this play.

75. Owen (ed.), 82, suggests that Ion might exit at 183 and return in time for the chorus' questions at 219ff, and Verall (ed.), 18–20, gives those stage directions. There is no reason, however, for these assumptions: exits are almost always signalled or evident from subsequent action. See also Mastronarde, 32–4, on this and similar scenes.

76. On what the *audience* saw of this fine description, see Hourmouziades, 55–6.

77. See above, Chapter 4, for the circumstances of this announcement.

78. Typically, the entering character initiates the dialogue; see above, Chapter 2. The contrast between Kreousa's and the others' entrances is made explicit by Ion at 244ff.

79. His entrance is not unprepared for, however; see 299ff.

80. Xouthos' alien status is referred to many times in the play, from Hermes' prologue (63) on (see, e.g., 290 and 592, where he is described with the adjective *epaktós*, and 702, 721ff), and at the end of the play he is excluded from the divine explanation and prophecy and the shared secrets of Ion and Kreousa.

81. See Bain, above n. 19, 37–8. Xouthos, of course, does not hear these words; see above, Chapter 3 n. 7.

82. Xouthos exits into the *skene*, representing the temple, Kreousa exits to an off-stage altar (see Xouthos' order at 422–24), and Ion to the holy fountains (cf. 435–6). The off-stage areas reached by the *parodoi* are not clearly defined (see Hourmouziades, 134–5), and so it can only be *suggested* that Kreousa and Ion exit in separate directions. A.P. Burnett in her translation of the play (Englewood Cliffs, N.J. 1970) makes the same suggestion; in the Budé translation they are both sent off 'stage left'.

83. Proposed by Wilamowitz (ed.), 110.

84. Admetos employs it referring to Alkestis' corpse being carried away by the servants (*Alk.* 610); but this is not, properly speaking, an entrance announcement.

85. The verbal connection between the end of the song and the following entrance was discussed above in Chapter 4.

86. There are many other entrances that depict slowness and difficulty of

walking — e.g., the old man's at *El.* 487ff, the chorus' at *Her.* 107ff, and Teiresias' at *Phoin.* 834ff.

87. Nowhere else in tragedy does the chorus break its pledge of silence. See Barrett (ed.), *Hipp.*, 294.

88. This intervention by the chorus, unique in tragedy, propels the events of the second half of the drama and Apollo's rescue therein, as Athene explains (1563ff).

89. Taplin, above n. 60, 55, proposes this.

90. Kreousa declares that she is being pursued (*diōkómestha*, 1250) and announces that the men after her are hastening (*epeígontai*, 1258). On the speed of entrances, see the bibliography cited at Taplin, 147 n. 2, and for rapid successive entrances, Taplin, 351–2.

91. No account of the text and accompanying stage actions of 1261–81 is entirely satisfactory. For the most part I follow Mastronarde, 110–12, but, unlike M., I accept (tentatively) Diggle's deletion of 1275–8 ('On the 'Heracles' and 'Ion' of Euripides', *PCPS* n.s. 20 (1974), 28–30). For other recent attempts to solve the problems of this scene, see D. Bain, 'Euripides, *Ion* 1261–81', *CQ* n.s. 29 (1979), 263–7, and *Masters, Servants, and Orders in Greek Tragedy* (Manchester 1981), 35–6, and Taplin, above n. 60, 187 n. 9.

92. In her review of Mastronarde (*CP* 77 (1982), 361–4), N. Rabinowitz objects that 'there is no dramatic or psychological reason for Creusa to linger'. The dramatic reason I suggest in the text. There might also be a psychological reason — fear (suggested obliquely by M. at 111). A close parallel for movements 'slowed down' by fear is *Hel.* 541ff, where, although Helen's return to the tomb and the escape from the not-recognised Menelaos is said to be at a fast pace (see 543, 546), she does not reach it until 556. Mastronarde, 111 n. 52, cites this parallel, but does not mention the fear expressed in both cases.

93. See Taplin, above n. 60, 72–3, on the significance of this act, although he does not think she reaches the altar until 1285.

94. This entrance was discussed above in Chapter 3.

95. As observed above in Chapter 3, she is referred to earlier in the play (41–51, 318ff), but her entrance is still quite unexpected. Schmid-Stählin (I.3, 554) calls her entrance the 'first *deus ex machina*'.

96. Taplin, above n. 50, holds that only silences that are commented on or referred to when they are broken are significant; obviously I disagree here. On this scene, see H. Strohm, *Euripides: Interpretationen zur dramatischen Form* Zetemata 15 (Munich 1957) 30–1.

97. On the parallels between these two scenes, esp. the verbal echoes, see Taplin, above n. 60, 137–8.

98. Advances which Ion takes as pederasty; see Taplin, above n. 60, 138.

99. See Burnett, above n. 70, 95 and 102 n. 26.

100. Athene's entrance, however, is not entirely unprepared for: twice, not too long before this appearance, Kreousa swears by Athene that Apollo is Ion's father (1478, 1528–9), as Mastronarde observes in 'Iconography and Imagery in Euripides' *Ion*', *CSCA* 8 (1975), 170. Also Athene's entrance can be seen as a very belated response to the chorus' plea in the first stasimon that she come. The surprise of this entrance was discussed above in Chapter 3.

6 APPENDIX: UNINTERRUPTED STROPHIC SONGS

In modifying Hourmouziades' formulation of the conventions that obtain for entrance announcements, Hamilton (1978) criticised him for assuming, *inter alia*, 'that it made no difference whether a "choral song" is strophic or astrophic, sung by the chorus alone or by the chorus with actor' (68–9). As is evident from Hamilton's study, the distinction between strophic and astrophic is fundamentally correct, but should we further distinguish between choral and not purely choral strophic songs?

Euripides has only a very few examples of the relevant sequence, a not purely choral uninterrupted song followed directly by an entrance. (An uninterrupted strophic song is one in which no non-responding lines, with the exception, of course, of an epode, intervene between the beginning and end of the song.) Several apparent examples are vitiated by either being interrupted by non-responding lines (e.g. *Hek.* 154ff and *Ion* 184ff) or being followed by such lines *before* the entrance (e.g. *El.* 167ff). Of genuine examples there are at most four. Jason arrives unannounced at *Med.* 1293, directly following an uninterrupted strophic song shared by the chorus and the children from within. (Hamilton in his appendix mistakenly lists this song as purely choral.) Theseus' final entrance in *Hik.* would provide another example, if he arrives at 1165 after the duet between the main and subsidiary choruses, and if such a duet is considered not purely choral, since not only the main chorus is involved. The latter point is open to debate, but it is perhaps moot, since it seems probable that Theseus arrives earlier with the others at 1123, as suggested in Chapter 2. Talthybios' entrance at *Tro.* 235 follows an uninterrupted strophic song shared by Hekabe and the chorus, and it is announced (230–4). Two points must be remembered about this case. First, the announcement is in anapestic dimeter, a metre which for entrances almost always signals an entrance that is in some way slow, solemn, or impressive, a 'moving tableau', and such anapests frequently herald entrances even directly after choral stasima. (The reason, however, for the anapests here is not clear.) Secondly, there is no exit before the *parodos* in *Tro.* and this structural anomaly might account for the announcement of an entrance directly after it (see Chapter 2 for more on this entrance). Similarly, after the *parodos* of *Hypsipyle* (fr. 1 ii–iv) shared by Hypsipyle and the chorus, Amphiaraos is announced in anapests. According to Bond's (ed.) analysis, the song is strophic. But we should note that, although for choral stasima there is no difference between odes with and those without an epode in regard to entrance announcements, perhaps this is not true in lyric duets, where the epode, when sung by a single actor, as is the case in this play, might take on the nature of a monody. Also, perhaps for some reason this entrance should be considered a 'moving tableau', but this does not seem likely (see Chapter 2, n. 54).

The evidence from the other tragedians, although meagre, also points to the conclusion that there is no reason for distinguishing between purely choral and not purely choral songs with respect to entrance announcements. Aischylos has no pertinent examples, but Sophokles has a few. At *El.* 871 Chrysothemis enters without announcement directly after a strophic song shared by Elektra and chorus (and this entrance probably should not be considered surprising); and Theseus arrives without announcement at *OK* 1751 directly following a strophic lyric of Antigone, Ismene and the chorus. Earlier in *OK* (at 551) Theseus' arrival is announced although it follows immediately a strophic song sung by Oidipous and the chorus. All entrances in the play, however, are announced until the blind Oidipous leaves the stage. (Hamilton, 70 n. 25, also makes this observation.) Orestes' and Pylades' announced entrance at *El.* 1424 should not be considered in this context because the chorus makes the announcement with the opening words of the antistrophe, before it is clear that the song is, in fact, strophic. Aigisthos' entrance shortly thereafter (1422) is announced (1429ff) not, I think, because the preceding lyric is not purely choral, but because the lyric has been interrupted by the preceding entrance *within* the lyric (see the discussion of the messenger's entrance at *Hipp.* 1153 above in Chapter 2). Also the announcement falls within the lyric. Two of these examples offer support for my contention that purely choral and not purely choral lyrics are not to be distinguished in respect to entrance announcements, while the other two (*OK* 551 and *El.* 1442) can be readily explained on other grounds.

To put it simply, there is no example in tragedy of a not purely choral uninterrupted strophic song followed immediately by an announced entrance, where the announcement cannot be explained by other factors. There is, therefore, no reason to distinguish between purely choral and not purely choral strophic songs in regard to the conventions of entrance announcements. My formulation of the convention differs not greatly from Hamilton's (only very few cases, we have seen, are actually involved), but it seems more accurate in pointing to the *structure* alone of the lyric, not its participants, as the determining factor.

Taplin's thesis describes the structure of Greek tragedy in terms of 'act-dividing songs', which include astrophic and interrupted ones. To a great extent the conventions of entrance announcements dovetail with the structural patterns of tragedy as defined by Taplin, but they do differ in this regard: the songs after which one can expect an *unannounced* arrival are those that are uninterrupted and strophic.

BIBLIOGRAPHY

1. Texts and Commentaries of Euripides Cited or Referred to in the Text

Austin, C. *Nova Fragmenta Euripidea in Papyris Reperta* (Berlin 1968)
Barrett, W.S. *Euripides: Hippolytos* (Oxford 1964)
Benedetto, V. di *Euripidis Orestes* (Florence 1965)
Biehl, W. *Euripides: Orestes* (Berlin 1965)
―――*Euripides: Troades* (Leipzig 1970)
Bond, G.W. *Euripides: Heracles* (Oxford 1981)
―――*Euripides: Hypsipyle* (Oxford 1963)
Burnett, A.P. (trans.) *Euripides: Ion* (Englewood Cliffs, N.J. 1970)
Campbell, A.Y. *Euripides: Helena* (Liverpool 1950)
Collard, C. *Euripides: Supplices*, 2 vols. (Groningen 1975)
Daitz, S.G. *Euripides: Hecuba* (Leipzig 1973)
Dale, A.M. *Euripides: Alcestis* (Oxford 1954)
―――*Euripides: Helen* (Oxford 1967)
Denniston, J.D. *Euripides: Electra* (Oxford 1939)
Diggle, J. *Euripidis Fabulae*, vol. 2 (Oxford 1981)
―――*Euripides: Phaethon* (Cambridge 1970)
Dodds, E.R. *Euripides: Bacchae* [2] (Oxford 1960)
England, E.B. *The Iphigenia at Aulis of Euripides* (London and New York 1891)
Kambitsis, J. *L'Antiope d'Euripide* (Athens 1972)
Kannicht, R. *Euripides: Helena*, 2 vols. (Heidelberg 1969)
Lee, K.H. *Euripides: Troades* (London 1976)
Murray, G. *Euripidis Fabulae*, 3 vols. (Oxford 1902–13)
Nauck, A. *Euripidis Tragoediae*, vols. 1 and 2 (Leipzig 1895)
――― *Tragicorum Graecorum Fragments* [2] (1888) *Supplementum* adiecit B. Snell (Hildesheim 1964).
Owen, A.S. *Euripides: Ion* (Oxford 1939).
Page, D.L. *Greek Literary Papyri, vol. I* [2] (Cambridge, Mass. and London 1942)
―――*Euripides: Medea* (Oxford 1938)
Paley, F.A. *Euripides,* [2] 3 vols. (London 1872–80)
Parmentier, L. and Grégoire, H. *Euripide. Tome III: Héraclès, Les Suppliantes, Ion* (Paris 1950)
―――*Euripide. Tome IV: Les Troyennes, Iphigénie en Tauride, Électre* (Paris 1948)
Prinz, R. and Wecklein, N. *Euripidis Fabulae*, 3 vols. (Leipzig 1883–1902)
Roux, J. *Euripide: Les Bacchantes*, 2 vols. (Paris 1970–2)
Snell, B. *Euripides' Alexandros und andere Strassburger Papyri mit Fragmenten griechischer Dichter*, Hermes Einzelschriften 5 (Wiesbaden 1937)
Stevens, P.T. *Euripides: Andromache* (Oxford 1971)
Verrall, A.W. *The Ion of Euripides* (Cambridge 1890)
Wecklein, N. *Ausgewählte Tragödien des Euripides* (Leipzig 1879–1914)
Weil, H. *Sept tragédies d'Euripide* [2] (Paris 1913)
Wilamowitz-Moellendorff, U. von *Euripides: Herakles.* [2] 3 vols. Berlin 1895, rptd. (Darmstadt 1969).
―――*Euripides: Hippolytos* (Berlin 1891)
―――*Euripides: Ion* (Berlin 1926)

2. Works Cited

Adkins, A.W.H. 'Basic Greek Values in Euripides' *Hecuba* and *Hercules Furens*', *CQ* n.s. 16 (1966), 193–209

Aichele, K. *Die Epeisodien der griechischen Tragödie*. Diss. Tübingen 1966

Arnott, G. 'Euripides and the Unexpected' *G & R* Second Series 20 (1973), 49–64

Arnott, P. *Greek Scenic Conventions in the Fifth Century B.C.* (Oxford 1962)

Bain, D. *Actors and Audience: A Study of Asides and Related Conventions in Greek Drama* (Oxford 1977)

———'Euripides, *Ion* 1261–81', *CQ* n.s. 29 (1979), 263–7

———*Masters, Servants and Orders in Greek Tragedy: A Study of Some Aspects of Dramatic Technique and Convention* (Manchester 1981)

———'The Prologue of Euripides' *Iphigenia in Aulis*', *CQ* n.s. 27 (1977), 10–26

Barlow, S. *The Imagery of Euripides* (London 1971)

Bodensteiner, E. *Szenische Fragen über den Ort des Auftretens und Abgehens von Schauspielern und Chor im griechischen Drama*, Jahrb. f. class. Philol. Suppl. Bd. 19 (1893), 637–808

Burnett, A.P. *Catastrophe Survived: Euripides' Plays of Mixed Reversal* (Oxford 1971)

———'Human Resistance and Divine Persuasion in Euripides' *Ion*', *CP* 57 (1962), 89–103

———'*Trojan Women* and the Ganymede Ode', *YCS* 25 (1977), 291–316

Carrière, J. *Le choeur secondaire dans le drame grec, sur une ressource méconnue de la scène antique* (Paris 1977)

Chalk, H. '*Aretē* and *bia* in Euripides' *Herakles*', *JHS* 82 (1962), 7–18

Collinge, N.E. 'Medea *Ex Machina*', *CP* 57 (1962), 170–2

Conacher, D. *Euripidean Drama: Myth, Theme and Structure* (Toronto 1967)

Dale, A.M. *Collected Papers* (Cambridge 1969)

Diggle, J. 'On the "Heracles" and "Ion" of Euripides', *PCPS* n.s. 20 (1974), 3–36

Diller, H. (rev.), E. Fraenkel, 'Zu den Phoenissen des Euripides', *SBAW* (Munich 1963) Heft 1, *Gnomon* 36 (1964), 641–50

Duchemin, J. *L'AGΩN dans la tragédie grecque*² (Paris 1968)

Else, G. *Aristotle's Poetics: The Argument* (Cambridge, Mass. 1957)

Erbse, H. 'Beiträge zum Verständnis der euripideischen "Phoenissen"', *Philologus* 110 (1966), 1–34

———'Euripides' "Andromache"', *Hermes* 94 (1966) 276–97

Fontenrose, J. 'Poseidon in the *Troades*', *Agon* 1 (1967), 135–41

———'A Response to Wilson's Reply on the *Troades*', *Agon* 2 (1968), 69–71

Fraenkel, E. 'Zu den Phonissen des Euripides', *SBAW* (Munich 1963), Heft 1

Friedrich, W. *Euripides und Diphilos: Zur Dramaturgie der Spätform*, Zetemata 5 (Munich 1953)

Gould, J. 'Hiketeia', *JHS* 93 (1973), 74–103

Graeber, P. *De poetarum Atticorum arte scaenica quaestiones quinque*. Diss. Göttingen 1911.

Gregory, J. 'Euripides' *Alcestis*', *Hermes* 107 (1979) 259–70

———'Euripides' *Heracles*', *YCS* 25 (1977), 259–75

Hamilton, R. 'Announced Entrances in Greek Tragedy', *HSCP* 82 (1978), 63–82

———'Prologue Prophecy and Plot in Four Plays of Euripides', *AJP* 99 (1978), 277–302

Handley, E.W. *The Dyskolos of Menander* (Cambridge, Mass. 1965)

Harms, C. *De introitu personarum in Euripide et novae comoediae fabulis*. Diss. Göttingen 1914

Helg, W. *Das Chorlied der griechischen Tragödie in seinem Verhältnis zur*

Handlung. Diss Oberwintherthur, Zürich 1950

Henrichs, A. 'Zur *Meropis*: Herakles' Löwenfell und Athenas zweite Haut', *ZPE* 27 (1975), 69–75

——'Human Sacrifice in Greek Religion: Three Case Studies' in *Le Sacrifice dans l'antiquité*, Entretiens sur l'antiquité classique, 27 (Vandoeuvres-Geneva 1981 195–242)

Hourmouziades, N. *Production and Imagination in Euripides: Form and Function of the Scenic Space*, Greek Society for Humanistic Studies, Second Series, vol. 5 (Athens 1965)

Jouan, F. *Euripide et les légendes des chants cypriens* (Paris 1966)

Knox, B. 'The *Medea* of Euripides', *YCS* 25 (1977), 193–225 = *Word and Action: Essays on the Ancient Theater* (Baltimore and London 1979) 295–322

——(rev.), A.P. Burnett, *Catastrophe Survived: Euripides' Plays of Mixed Reversal* (Oxford 1971), *CP* 67 (1972), 270–9 = *Word and Action: Essays on the Ancient Theater* (Baltimore and London 1979), 329–42

Köhler, W. *Die Versbrechung bei den griechischen Tragikern.* Diss. Giessen, Darmstadt 1913

Kranz, W. *Stasimon: Untersuchungen zu Form und Gehalt der griechischen Tragödie* (Berlin 1933)

Kubo, M. 'The Norm of Myth: Euripides' *Electra*', *HSCP* 71 (1966), 15–31

Lattimore, R. *Story Patterns in Greek Tragedy* (Ann Arbor 1964)

Leo, F. *Der Monolog im Drama: Ein Beitrag zur griechisch-römischen Poetik*, Abh. Ges. Wiss Göttingen phil-hist. Kl. N. F. 10, 5 (Berlin 1908)

Lesky, A. *Greek Tragic Poetry* (New Haven 1983), trans. M. Dillon, *Die Tragische Dichtung der Hellenen* [3] (Göttingen 1972)

Lucas, D. (ed.), *Aristotle: Poetics* (Oxford 1968)

Ludwig, W. *Sapheneia: Ein Beitrag zur Formkunst im Spätwerk des Euripides.* Diss. Tübingen 1954

Mastronarde, D. *Contact and Discontinuity: Some Conventions of Speech and Action on the Greek Tragic Stage* (Berkeley and Los Angeles 1979)

——'Iconography and Imagery in Euripides' *Ion*', *CSCA* 8 (1975) 163–76

Mills, S.P. 'The Sorrows of Medea', *CP* 75 (1980), 289–96

Möller, C. *Vom Chorlied bei Euripides.* Diss. Göttingen, Bottrop 1933.

Neitzel, H. *Die dramatische Funktion der Chorlieder in den Tragödien des Euripides.* Diss. Hamburg 1967.

Nestle, W. *Die Struktur des Eingangs in der attischen Tragödie* (Stuttgart 1930)

Norwood, G. *Essays on Euripidean Drama* (London 1954)

O'Neill, E., Jr. 'The Prologue of the *Troades* of Euripides', *TAPA* 72 (1941), 288–320.

Ortkemper, H. *Szenische Techniken des Euripides: Untersuchungen zur Gebärdensprache im antiken Theater.* Diss. Berlin 1969.

Page, D. *Actors' Interpolations in Greek Tragedy* (Oxford 1934)

Parry, H. *The Lyric Poems of Greek Tragedy* (Toronto and Sarasota 1978)

——'The Second Stasimon of Euripides' *Heracles* (637–700)', *AJP* 86 (1965), 363–74

Rabinowitz, N. (rev.), D. Mastronarde, *Contact and Discontinuity: Some Conventions of Speech and Action on the Greek Tragic Stage* (Berkeley and Los Angeles 1979), *CP* 77 (1982), 361–4

Rode, J. 'Das Chorlied' in W. Jens (ed.), *Die Bauformen der griechischen Tragödie* (Munich 1971) 85–115

de Romilly, J. *L'évolution du pathétique d'Eschyle à Euripide* (Paris 1961)

——*Time in Greek Tragedy* (Ithaca, N.Y. 1968)

Schadewaldt, W. *Monolog und Selbstgespräch: Untersuchungen zur Formgeschichte der griechischen Tragödie*, Neue Philologische Untersuchungen

2 (Berlin 1926)
Schmidt, H. 'Die Struktur des Eingangs' in W. Jens (ed.), *Die Bauformen der griechischen Tragödie* (Munich 1971) 1–46
Schmitt, W. *Der Deus ex machina bei Euripides*. Diss. Tübingen 1963.
Scodel, R. *The Trojan Trilogy of Euripides*, Hypomnemata 60 (Göttingen 1980)
Sifakis, G.M. 'Children in Greek Tragedy', *BICS* 26 (1979) 67–80
Spira, A. *Untersuchungen zum deus ex machina bei Sophokles und Euripides*. Diss. Frankfurt, Kallmünz 1960
Stanley-Porter, D.P. 'Who Opposes Theoclymenus?', *CP* 72 (1977), 45–8
Steidle, W. *Studien zum antiken Drama, unter besonderer Berücksichtigung des Bühnenspiels* (Munich 1968)
Strohm, H. *Euripides: Interpretationen zur dramatischen Form*, Zetemata 15 (Munich 1957)
Taplin, O. 'Aeschylean Silences and Silences in Aeschylus', *HSCP* 76 (1972), 57–97
_____'Did Greek Dramatists Write Stage Instructions?', *PCPS* n.s. 23 (1977), 121–32
_____*Greek Tragedy in Action* (Berkeley and Los Angeles 1978)
_____'Significant Actions in Sophocles' *Philoctetes'*, *GRBS* 12 (1971), 25–44
_____*The Stagecraft of Aeschylus: The Dramatic Use of Exits and Entrances in Greek Tragedy* (Oxford 1977)
Webster, T.B.L. 'Preparation and Motivation in Greek Tragedy', *CR* 47 (1933), 117–23
_____*The Tragedies of Euripides* (London 1967)
Whitman, C. *Euripides and the Full Circle of Myth* (Cambridge, Mass. 1974)
Wilson, J.R. 'An Interpolation in the Prologue of Euripides' *Troades'*, *GRBS* 8 (1967), 205–23
_____' "Poseidon in the *Troades*": A Reply' *Agon* 2 (1968), 66–8
Winnington-Ingram, R.P. *Euripides and Dionysus: An Interpretation of the Bacchae* (Cambridge 1948)
_____'Euripides: Poiētēs Sophos', *Arethusa* 2 (1969), 129–42
Wolff, C. 'The Design and Myth in Euripides' *Ion'*, *HSCP* 69 (1965), 169–94
Zuntz, G. *The Political Plays of Euripides* (Manchester 1955)
Note: I have been unable to see E. García Novo, *La entrada de los personajes y su anuncio en la tragedia griega: un estudio de técnica teatral* (Madrid 1981).

INDEX LOCORUM

DATE DUE